A Diocesan Research Guide for Family Historians

U.S.
CATHOLIC
Sources

Compiled by Virginia Humling

Humling, Virginia Erickson
U.S. Catholic sources: a diocesan research guide for family
historians/ compiled by Virginia Humling
         p.   cm.
ISBN 0-916489-60-4
1. Church records and registers-United States-Directories.
2. United States-Genealogy-Archival resources-Directories
3. Catholics-United States-Genealogy-Archival resources-
Directories   I. Title.
CD3065.H86   1995
026 .28273-dc20   95-25259
                          CIP

Copyright 1995
Ancestry.com
P.O. Box 990
Orem, Utah 84059

First printing 1995
10 9 8 7 6 5 4 3

Printed in the United States of America

CONTENTS

Contents

Contents

Contents

Contents

U.S. Catholic Sources

INTRODUCTION

The information presented in this guide was compiled from questionnaires mailed to all Roman Catholic dioceses within the United States. The response was gratifying, with all but three of the dioceses responding. My thanks are extended to all of the diocesan personnel who so graciously answered my questionnaires, letters, and telephone calls. The amount of data provided in the responses varied. Some contained detailed information on access to records, search procedures, fees, etc. Many of the dioceses simply stated that all records within the diocese are maintained at the parish level; such a response usually does not indicate an unwillingness to be helpful to researchers, but simply that sacramental records within the diocese are not centralized at the chancery offices. In some such cases, I followed up with a telephone call to clarify search procedures in those dioceses. Usually, where the records are not available at the diocesan level, chancery personnel are willing to try to help locate a parish where records might be found. They may then forward the request to the appropriate parish; some will provide the address of the church to which researchers may direct their inquiries.

For many of the dioceses, I have included information on Catholic newspapers. Generally, the more recent papers do not include obituaries or marriage announcements. Newspapers that were published in the nineteenth century and into the early parts of the twentieth century often included such news, though very few of them are indexed for marriages and obituaries. Microfilm and hard copies of many of these publications are available to researchers at various state libraries and historical societies, and often at the newspaper offices (if they still exist). Newspaper collections can also be found at many Catholic colleges and universities; sometimes these are available through interlibrary loan.

Some questionnaires were also sent to genealogical societies and state and county libraries. The response was not as great as I had hoped, but such information is included in each state section. Again,

I am grateful to those who responded, and I welcome pertinent additions. Several of the libraries listed have extensive genealogical collections. Because I requested items specifically Catholic in nature, I have tried to include only those items. From a genealogical perspective, the most valuable records for the researcher with a Catholic heritage are the records that pertain to the sacraments of baptism and matrimony. Baptismal and marriage records are maintained in chronological order (by date, then by surname) in registers housed at the parish level. The registers of churches that have been closed are usually maintained at chancery or diocesan archives. Baptismal records usually include the following information: the date of baptism; the child's full name; the full names of the parents, often including the mother's maiden surname; the names of the godparents or sponsors of the child; and the signature of the officiating priest. In areas where the Church was of Spanish origin, early records may also reflect the Spanish policy of including detailed information on the grandparents of the newly baptized infant.

Marriage registers usually include the following information: the date of the marriage; the full names of the bride (maiden surname) and groom; the names of the two official witnesses; and the signature of the officiating priest. Sometimes date and place of birth are also included. Traditionally, marriages within the Catholic church are celebrated in the bride's parish, so record searches should begin there.

Records related to death and burial often include the following information: name of the deceased, often including the maiden surname; age at death; date of death/and or burial; place of burial; whether the sacrament of Extreme Unction was administered (Penance and Eucharist); and the name of an informant, often a relative. Sometimes the deceased's place of birth is also recorded. Catholic cemeteries are maintained at both the diocesan and the parish level, and cemetery records are kept by the organization incorporating the cemetery. An excellent source of information on cemeteries located within the particular dioceses is *The Official Catholic Directory*, published annually by P.J. Kenedy and Sons. The directory can be found in all diocesan chancery offices, in many parishes, and in the reference section of most of the larger public library systems.

Records pertaining to the sacraments of First Communion and Confirmation are also included in some diocesan archives. Generally, however, they are not as useful to researchers. First Communion is administered at the parish, usually around the age of seven. These records often include only the date and a list of communicants. Confirmation records often comprise only a list of those candidates confirmed (which, until recently, occurred around the age of thirteen). The name of the candidate's sponsor may also be recorded.

The most common bit of advice offered to family historians by diocesan personnel is: Do your initial research before requesting records from the parishes or dioceses! Most parishes and diocesan offices are not staffed to perform research for individuals. Research often requires time away from the duties involved in the daily business of the parish or diocesan office. The following is a suggested list of items needed for a successful search:

1. The full name of the individual whose record you are requesting. For baptisms, also include the parents' full names. For marriages, include the bride's maiden surname and the groom's full name.
2. The type of record you wish researched (baptism, first communion, confirmation, marriage, and/or death.)
3. The approximate date (within three to five years) on which the sacrament would have been performed.
4. The parish in which the sacrament was administered. If the exact parish is not known, the address or neighborhood of the individual con-

cerned may help to determine the parish. Ethnic information may also be a clue to the parish, as parishes were often organized on ethnic or national lines in the nineteenth century. If you are researching a marriage record, the bride's parish or her parents' address at the time of the wedding is needed.

Information concerning fees is listed for each diocese. Many dioceses have no set fees, but donations are usually accepted to defray the cost of research time. (Most government agencies require a set amount for records and research, prepaid.)

Researchers who have priests and other clergy in their families may want to check the archives of the motherhouses of those orders. The religious orders usually kept very good family information on their members. Again, *The Official Catholic Directory* is an excellent starting point. It lists the names of all religious orders currently operating within the various dioceses. If the order still exists, the records will reside with the order. The diocesan archives is often the depository for the records of orders which are now defunct.

I have departed a bit from this guide's format in the case of the Archdiocese for Military Services, U.S.A. located in Silver Spring, Maryland. This archdiocese maintains the records of sacraments performed on U.S. military bases worldwide. For the reader's convenience, this archdiocese is described both under Maryland and near the end of the guide.

Interestingly, researchers with a Catholic heritage will sometimes have more success in their record searches through the Genealogical Society of Utah. The Genealogical Society of Utah maintains the largest genealogical collection in existence at the Family History Library of The Church of Jesus Christ of Latter-day Saints (LDS Church) in Salt Lake City. These records are open to the public at the Family History Library and through the more than four hundred LDS family history centers throughout the United States, Canada, Mexico, and

Europe. The society has microfilmed the records of several Catholic doiceses in their entirety, as well as the records of many other individual Catholic churches and cemeteries. Copies of the microfilms maintained at the Family History Library in Salt Lake City may be borrowed through family history centers for a nominal fee. Remember that all church records copied by the society (regardless of denomination) are filed by state, county, and then town in the Family History Library catalog. The last section of this guide is a list of the diocese whose records have been microfilmed by the society.

My purpose in creating this guide to the public is to increase the ease of locating the records that are a precious part of our Catholic heritage. In addition, my hope for those still practicing the "faith of our fathers" (and mothers!) is that, in reflecting on the faith journeys of those who came before us, we will appreciate the debt of gratitude for what has been so faithfully handed down to us. Our journeys are truly connected.

Happy searching!
Virginia Humling

ALABAMA

ARCHDIOCESE OF MOBILE

400 Government Street
P.O. Box 1966
Mobile, AL 36633
Telephone: (334) 434–1585

AREA INCLUDED IN DIOCESE:

Autauga, Baldwin, Barbour, Bullock, Butler, Choctaw, Clarke, Coffee, Conecuh, Covington, Crenshaw, Dale, Dallas, Elmore, Escambia, Geneva, Henry, Houston, Lee, Lowndes, Macon, Mobile, Monroe, Montgomery, Pike, Russell, Washington, and Wilcox counties in southern Alabama.

Baptismal, marriage, and burial records are retained in the archives at the chancery.

FEES:

Archival research, $7.50 per hour; copies of baptismal, marriage, and/or burial records, $5.00 each; if certified, $7.50 each.

DIOCESE OF BIRMINGHAM

P.O. Box 12047
Birmingham, AL 35202–2047
Telephone: (205) 833–0175

AREA INCLUDED IN DIOCESE:

Bibb, Blount, Calhoun, Chambers, Cherokee, Chilton, Clay, Cleburne, Colbert, Coosa, Cullman, DeKalb, Etowah, Fayette, Franklin, Greene, Hale, Jackson, Jefferson, Lamar, Lauderdale, Lawrence, Limestone, Madison, Marengo, Marion, Marshall, Morgan, Perry, Pickens, Randolph, St. Clair, Shelby, Sumter, Talladega, Tallapoosa, Tuscaloosa, Walker, and Winston counties in northern Alabama.

All sacramental records are maintained at the parish level. Baptismal certificates, when requested for Social Security purposes, etc., are issued by the parish of origin.

FEES:

Determined by the parish.

ADDITIONAL ALABAMA RESOURCES:

STATE OF ALABAMA

Dept. of Archives and History
624 Washington Ave.
Montgomery, AL 36130–3601

COLLECTION INCLUDES:

- Cathedral of the Immaculate Conception (Mobile)
- Family Records, 1700–1860
- Scattered issues of Mobile and Birmingham Catholic newspapers in originals
- Local Catholic Cemetery gravestone transcriptions and funeral home records
- Items pertaining to Catholic education in Alabama (yearbooks, student and faculty lists), scattered localities and dates

NORTH CENTRAL ALABAMA GENEALOGICAL SOCIETY

c/o Hermenia Voss Basch
1425 Mitchell Rd. N.W.
Cullman, AL 35055

COLLECTION INCLUDES:

- Early Catholic records, including baptisms, marriages, deaths, and cemetery records for Cullman County and Warrior Church, Jefferson County

HERITAGE ROOM

Huntsville-Madison County Public Library
915 Monroe St.
P.O. Box 443
Huntsville, AL 35804

COLLECTION INCLUDES:

- Brief information about St. Mary's School and Church (Huntsville)
- Family File collection of unpublished information arranged by surname

ALASKA

ARCHDIOCESE OF ANCHORAGE

225 Cordova St.
Anchorage, AK 99501

MAILING ADDRESS:
P.O. Box 2239
Anchorage, AK 99510
Telephone: (907) 258–7898

ARCHIVIST:
Br. Charles McBride

AREA INCLUDED IN DIOCESE:
The old territorial Third Judicial Division, for which the boundary extended northwest from the Canadian border along the crest of the Alaska range to Mt. McKinley, thence southwesterly to Cape Newenham and west along the 58th parallel north of the Probolof Islands.

Requests for records should be directed to the parish where the sacrament was performed. The archdiocese can be helpful in locating a parish if sufficient information is provided.

FEES:
None

DIOCESE OF FAIRBANKS

Chancery Office
1316 Peger Road
Fairbanks, AK 99709
Telephone: (907) 474–0753

ARCHIVIST:
Rev. Francis E. Mueller, S.J.

AREA INCLUDED IN DIOCESE:
All of the state of Alaska north of the old Territorial Third Judicial Division.

Request sacramental records from parishes, where they are kept. If a parish has problems locating the record, the chancery will assist, as the data is also retained there for security and backup purposes.

FEES:
If the record is for sacramental purposes—e.g., for a person preparing to receive First Communion or for a marriage, there is no charge. For genealogical research the fee is $5.00.

DIOCESE OF JUNEAU

419 Sixth St., No. 200
Juneau, AK 99801
Telephone: (907) 586–2227

AREA INCLUDED IN DIOCESE:

The entire southeastern part of Alaska, known as
the First Judicial District.

The Diocese of Juneau keeps records of the missions and outlying areas and the sacraments performed there. Parish records within the diocese are maintained at the parish level. The diocese will refer researchers to the church where the sacrament took place for copies of records.

FEES:

Determined by the parish.

CATHOLIC NEWSPAPER:

The Inside Passage
419 Sixth St.
Juneau, AK 99801

Est. 1970. May be researched at the newspaper offices by appointment.

ADDITIONAL ALASKA RESOURCES:

ALASKA STATE LIBRARY/HISTORICAL SOCIETY

P.O. Box 110571
Juneau, AK 99811–0571

COLLECTION INCLUDES:

• Funeral records for Juneau, 1898–1964
• A general list of the Evergreen Cemetery (Juneau), which includes a Catholic section, 1880s through 1980s
• Father Joseph Bernard, photographs of Catholic missions, 1906–1916
• Microfilm of Oregon Province Archives of the Society of Jesus, Alaska Missions Collection, 1880s through 1950s

ARCHIVES/ALASKA & POLAR REGIONS DEPT.

E.E. Rasmuson Library
University of Alaska/Fairbanks
Fairbanks, AK 99775–1005

COLLECTION INCLUDES:

• Microfilm of the Oregon Province Archives of the Society of Jesus, Alaska Missions Collection
• Funeral records of Hosea H. Ross Funeral Home, 1918–1941 (Many entries include notes on "Catholic burial or plot.")
• Extensive records for the Russian Orthodox Catholic Church in Alaska

ARIZONA

DIOCESE OF PHOENIX

400 East Monroe
Phoenix, AZ 85004–2376
Telephone: (602) 257–0030

AREA INCLUDED IN DIOCESE:

Maricopa, Mohave, Yavapai and Coconino counties (does not include the territorial boundaries of the Navajo Indian Reservation) and Pinal County (the portion of land known as the Gila River Indian Reservation).

The first parish established in what is now the Diocese of Phoenix was in Prescott in 1877. Locating records created prior to that time can be difficult. Supplying precise information (names, dates, addresses) will increase the possibility of locating any records. Send requests for information or certificates to the parish of origin, if known.

FEES:

Small donations are appreciated.

DIOCESE OF TUCSON

192 South Stone Ave.
Box 31
Tucson, AZ 85702
Telephone: (520) 792–3410

Archives
8800 East 22nd St.
Tucson, AZ 85710
Telephone: (520) 886–5223

ARCHIVIST:

Donald P. Brosnan, C.R.M.

AREA INCLUDED IN DIOCESE:

Cochise, Gila, Graham, Greenlee, La Paz, Pima, Pinal, Santa Cruz, and Yuma counties.

Many sacramental records are found at the parish level. Consolidation in the diocesan archives is under consideration. Direct requests for information or certificates to the parish of origin, if known. A few very early sacramental records for the diocese are on microfilm at the Arizona State Library in Phoenix.

FEES:

$2.50 per certificate. A donation is asked for research.

DIOCESAN HISTORY:

A two-volume history of the diocese, *Salpointe and Shepherds in the Desert* (Odie B. Faulk, ed. 1978), is available from the diocesan offices for $25.00 and postage.

ADDITIONAL ARIZONA RESOURCES:

ARIZONA STATE LIBRARY
STATE CAPITOL BLDG., NO. F13

Phoenix, AZ 85007–2812

COLLECTION INCLUDES:

- Records of Church Women United in Arizona, 1954–1973
- *Catholic Sun*, Nov.-Dec. 1985, 1986–1982 (hard copies only)
- Citizens' cemetery records, 1897–1907, Prescott. Contains names of individuals leasing plats for $2.50 a year in 1927
- Microfilm of fragmentary baptismal, marriage, and burial books for the Diocese of Tucson. Mission Los Santos Angeles de Guevavi (variously called San Gabriel, San Gabriel y San Rafael, and San Miguel), Jesuit, 1739–1767

- Mission San Jose de Tumacacori (until ca. 1771 Los Santos Angeles de Guevavi), Franciscan, one reel
- Catholic directory of the Diocese of Tucson, 1936
- Yearbooks for St. Joseph's Academy, 1923, 1924

PHOENIX PUBLIC LIBRARY

12 East McDowell
Phoenix, AZ 85004

COLLECTION INCLUDES:

- Three volume set of Arizona death records—an index compiled from mortuary, cemetery and church records.

ARKANSAS

DIOCESE OF LITTLE ROCK

2415 North Tyler Street
P.O. Box 7239—Forest Park Station
Little Rock, AR 72217
Telephone: (501) 664–0340

ARCHIVIST:
Sr. Catherine Markey, OSB

AREA INCLUDED IN DIOCESE:
Entire state of Arkansas

Sacramental records for existing parishes are maintained at the parish level, where certificates are issued. Pre-diocesan records (prior to 1843) are located at the Chancery.

FEES:
Determined by the parish. There is a fee of $5.00 for each certified copy of a pre-diocesan record from the chancery.

DIOCESAN HISTORY:
The History of Catholicity in Arkansas (1925) by the Historical Commission of the Diocese of Little Rock.

Mission and Memory: A History of the Catholic Church in Arkansas (1993) by James M. Woods is available though the diocesan offices for $30.00 and $2.00 shipping and handling (per book).

ADDITIONAL ARKANSAS RESOURCES:

ARKANSAS HISTORY COMMISSION

One Capitol Mall
Little Rock, AR 72201

COLLECTION INCLUDES:
- Cemetery records for many part of Arkansas
- Catholic newspapers and Arkansas newspapers from 1819 to the present

SOUTHWEST ARKANSAS REGIONAL ARCHIVES

Old Washington Historic State Park
Washington, AR 71862

COLLECTION INCLUDES:
- Extensive material from the twelve counties that formed the original Hempstead County of 1819 (Columbia, Hempstead, Howard, Lafayette, Little River, Miller, Nevada, Ouachita, Pike, Polk, Sevier, and Union), including cemetery records
- Marriage records: Arkansas marriage records, 1808–1835; Columbia Co., 1852–1865; Hempstead Co., 1817–1937; Lafayette Co., 1828–1907; Nevada Co., 1852–1865; Sevier Co., 1829–1865; Union Co. 1829–1875
- Small manuscript file which includes church histories and funeral notices
- Family history file

ARKANSAS HISTORY AND GENEALOGY ROOM

Greene County Library
120 North 12th St.
Paragould, AR 72450

COLLECTION INCLUDES:
- *Cemeteries of Greene County, Arkansas*, a gravestone index published by the Greene County Historical and Genealogical Society. Available for purchase or use at the Greene County Library; includes St. Mary's Cemetery in Paragould.

RANDOLPH COUNTY LIBRARY

111 West Everett
Pocahontas, AR 72455

COLLECTION INCLUDES:
- Gravestone inscriptions of St. Paul and St. John Cemeteries, Randolph Co.

ARCHDIOCESE OF LOS ANGELES

3423 Wilshire Blvd.
Los Angeles, CA 90010–2241
Telephone: (213) 637–7000

AREA INCLUDED IN ARCHDIOCESE:

Los Angeles, Santa Barbara, and Ventura counties.

Sacramental records for the Archdiocese of Los Angeles are maintained at the parishes in which they were performed. Requests should be directed to the parish of origin. The archdiocese is not staffed to perform genealogical research.

FEES:

Determined by the parish.

DIOCESAN HISTORY:

Century of Fulfillment: The Roman Catholic Church in Southern California (1990) by Rev. Msgr. Francis J. Weber.

CATHOLIC NEWSPAPER:

The Tidings
1530 West 9th Street
Los Angeles, CA 90015

Est. 1895. Microfilm copies (1895 to present) are located at the Los Angeles Public Library.

ARCHIVES OF THE ARCHDIOCESE OF SAN FRANCISCO

320 Middlefield Road
Menlo Park, CA 94025
Telephone: (650) 328–6502

AREA INCLUDED IN ARCHDIOCESE:

Marin, San Francisco, and San Mateo counties.

The archives house copies of sacramental records for all parishes within the Archdiocese of San Francisco. In addition, the archives holds microfilm copies for the dioceses of Oakland, San Jose, Santa Rosa, and Stockton. The archives is open to researchers; con-firmation of hours is suggested before visiting. The archives is not staffed to perform genealogical research. Written requests must include accurate information so that the record can be retrieved without additional research. Certificates are issued by the parish of origin.

FEES:

Copying fees only at the archives. Fees for certificates are determined by the parish.

DIOCESE OF FRESNO

P.O. Box 1668
1550 N. Fresno St.
Fresno, CA 93717
Telephone: (209) 488–7400

AREA INCLUDED IN DIOCESE:

Fresno, Inyo, Kern, Kings, Madera, Mariposa, Merced, and Tulare counties.

Sacramental records are maintained at the parish level. Some records are also on file in the diocesan archives.

FEES:

There are no set fees, but donations are appreciated.

DIOCESE OF MONTEREY

580 Fremont Street
P.O. Box 2048
Monterey, CA 93942
Telephone: (408) 373–4345

ARCHIVIST:

Br. John F. O'Brien, CFX

AREA INCLUDED IN DIOCESE:

Monterey, San Benito, San Luis Obispo, and Santa Cruz counties.

Sacramental records are maintained at the parish level, where certificates are issued. Some genealogical sources for the area can be found at the Monterey Bay History Center, Seaside, CA, 93955. Many parish records are also on file at the diocesan archives. Researchers will be sent an application on request. The diocesan staff prefers to perform the research; researchers can be accommodated only individually, by appointment, as space at the archives is limited.

FEES:
$10.00 per copy.

DIOCESE OF OAKLAND

2900 Lakeshore Ave.
Oakland, CA 94610
Telephone: (510) 893–4711

AREA INCLUDED IN DIOCESE:
Alameda and Contra Costa counties.

Microfilm of early sacramental records for the diocese is housed in the Chancery Archives of the Archdiocese of San Francisco, 320 Middlefield Rd., Menlo Park, CA, 94025. Certificates are issued by the parish of origin.

FEES:
Determined by the parish.

CATHOLIC NEWSPAPER:
The Catholic Voice
2918 Lakeshore Ave.
Oakland, CA 94610

Est. 1963. Has never carried obituaries or marriage announcements. *The Monitor* (San Francisco) covered the area until 1962 (no longer published). *The Monitor* is on file at the Graduate Theological Union at Berkeley.

DIOCESE OF ORANGE

2811 East Villa Real Dr.
Orange, CA 92666
Telephone: (714) 282–3000

AREA INCLUDED IN DIOCESE:
Orange County.

Sacramental records for the Diocese of Orange are maintained at the parish level.

FEES:
Determined by the parish.

CATHOLIC NEWSPAPER:
The Diocese of Orange Bulletin
2811 East Villa Real Dr.
Orange, CA 92667

Est. 1977. Prior to 1977, the area was covered by *Tidings* (Archdiocese of Los Angeles). *The Bulletin* may be inspected at the newspaper offices by appointment.

DIOCESE OF SACRAMENTO–ARCHIVES

P.O. Box 254647
Sacramento, CA 95825
Telephone: (916) 733–0288

ARCHIVIST:
Rev. William Breault, S.J.

AREA INCLUDED IN DIOCESE:
Amador, Butte, Colusa, El Dorado, Glenn, Lassen, Modoc, Nevada, Placer, Plumas, Sacramento, Shasta, Sierra, Siskiyou, Solano, Sutter, Tehama, Trinity, Yolo, and Yuba counties.

Sacramental records for the diocese are stored at the parish level, where certificates are issued. Some of the older books are housed at the archives. Requests should be directed to the parish of origin. If the parish is not known, the archivist may be of help. When a request at the archives involves more than simply looking up a name, a search sheet will be sent to the individual requesting information.

FEES:
Determined by the parish. There is a fee for extended searches carried out by the archives.

CATHOLIC NEWSPAPER:
Catholic Herald
5890 Newman Court
Sacramento, CA 95819

Est 1908. Microfilm for all years are housed at the newspaper offices and may be viewed by appointment.

DIOCESE OF SAN BERNARDINO
1450 North D St.
San Bernardino, CA 92405
Telephone: (909) 384–8200

ARCHIVIST:
Dr. R. Bruce Harvey (volunteer)

AREA INCLUDED IN DIOCESE:
San Bernardino and Riverside counties.

The Archives of the Diocese of San Bernardino is open to qualified researchers, with certain restrictions common to all diocesan archives. The collection includes the parish sacramental records from 1852 to the 1970s on microfilm and a tombstone "census" of some of the early Catholic cemeteries in the area. Sextons' records for the cemeteries do not exist, but the census provides a lot of information. Office hours: Tues. and Thurs., 10 A.M. to 4 P.M.

FEES:
Copies of baptismal certificates are available only at the parish level. The copying fee at the archives is 10 cents per page; microfilm reader copies are 15 cents per page.

DIOCESAN HISTORY:
Dr. R. Bruce Harvey has compiled a multi-volume history of the Diocese of San Bernardino. The series, titled *Readings in Diocesan Heritage*, chronicles the history of the Church in San Bernardino and Riverside counties. The outline of the series is as follows:

- *Volume 1. Hispanic Beginnings, 1774–1834*
- *Volume 2. Mission San Gabriel Expands Eastward, 1819–1834*
- *Volume 3. By the Gentle Waters: Agua Mansa and San Salvador Parish, 1842–1893*
- *Volume 4. St. Berardine's: Mother Church of Two Counties, 1862–1990*
- *Volume 5. The Catholic Church in San Bernardino County, 1819–1989*
- *Volume 6. Centennial History of the Catholic Church in Riverside County, 1886–1986*
- *Volume 7. Founders of the Faith*
- *Volume 8. St. Boniface Indian School, 1890–1978*
- *Volume 9. Catholic Institutions in the Diocese*
- *Volume 10. Ethnic Diversity in Diocesan History*
- *Volume 11. Most Reverend Charles Francis Buddy: First Bishop of San Diego, 1936–1966*
- *Volume 12. From a Mustard Seed: Heritage of the San Bernardino Diocese, 1774–1994*

The soft-bound volumes may be ordered through the Office of Archives, Diocese of San Bernardino. For more information, contact the diocese.

CATHOLIC NEWSPAPER:
The Inland Catholic
1441 North D St.
San Bernardino, CA 92405

Est. 1979. Prior to 1978 the area was covered by the *Southern Cross* out of San Diego. The paper may be inspected at the newspaper office by appointment.

DIOCESE OF SAN DIEGO
Archives
P.O. Box 85728
San Diego, CA 92186
Telephone: (619) 490–8200

ARCHIVIST:
Sr. Catherine Louise La Coste, CSJ

AREA INCLUDED IN DIOCESE:
Imperial and San Diego counties.

Sacramental records, beginning with 1769 Mission San Diego, are in the diocesan archives. The archives are not equipped for public use. Researchers should telephone ahead for appointments. Research is usually done by the archivist.

FEES:
There is no set fee, though donations are appreciated.

DIOCESAN HISTORY:
Most Reverend Charles Francis Buddy: First Bishop of San Diego 1936–1966 (1992) by Sr. Catherine Louise La Coste and Dr. R. Bruce Harley. Available through the Diocese of San Bernardino.

CATHOLIC NEWSPAPER:
The Southern Cross
P.O. Box 81869
San Diego, CA 92138

Est. 1913. Back issues are housed at the newspaper offices and can be researched by appointment. Not indexed.

DIOCESE OF SAN JOSE

900 Lafayette St. Suite 301
Santa Clara, CA 95050–4966
Telephone: (408) 983–0100

AREA INCLUDED IN DIOCESE:
Santa Clara County.

The Diocese of San Jose was created from the Archdiocese of San Francisco in 1981. Microfilm of sacramental records through 1962 are housed at the Archives of the Archdiocese of San Francisco (open to researchers). The diocese has no genealogical records. Any baptismal records must be obtained directly from the parish where the sacrament was performed.

FEES:
Determined by the parish.

DIOCESE OF SANTA ROSA

547 B St.
P.O. Box 1297
Santa Rosa, CA 95402
Telephone: (707) 545–7610

AREA INCLUDED IN DIOCESE:
Del Norte, Humboldt, Lake, Mendocino, Napa, and Sonoma counties.

Sacramental records in the Diocese of Santa Rosa are maintained at the parish level. Files in the Archives are not open for genealogical purposes. The Archives of the Archdiocese of San Francisco maintain microfilm copies of the records which are open to researchers.

DIOCESE OF STOCKTON

P.O. Box 4237
Stockton, CA 95204
Telephone: (209) 466–0636

AREA INCLUDED IN DIOCESE:
Alpine, Calaveras, Mono, San Joaquin, Stanislaus, and Tuolumne counties.

Sacramental records are maintained at the parish level. Requests for copies of records should be made to the parish of origin. The Archives of the Archdiocese of San Francisco maintain microfilm copies of the records which are open to researchers.

FEES:
Contributions are appreciated.

ADDITIONAL CALIFORNIA RESOURCES:

LOS ANGELES PUBLIC LIBRARY

630 West Fifth Street
Los Angeles, CA 90071

COLLECTION INCLUDES:

- *The Tidings*, 1895 to the present
- D.A.R. "Vital Records from Cemeteries in California"—includes thirty pages of burials in New Calvary Cemetery in Los Angeles. (This cemetery is now known as Calvary Cemetery. It has thousands of burials, and this listing is only a small portion of the whole. Researchers looking for Calvary Cemetery burial are advised to write to the cemetery manager at: 4201 Whittier Blvd., Los Angeles, CA, 90023.) Death records for Mission San Gabriel, 1774-1859, are also included in the volumes.
- D.A.R. baptismal records of Los Angeles County—includes baptisms at San Gabriel Mission, 1771–1859, and Plaza Church, 1826–1873
- Scattered parish histories

OAKLAND PUBLIC LIBRARY

125 14th St.
Oakland, CA 94612

COLLECTION INCLUDES:

- *The Catholic Voice*, 1978 to present
- D.A.R. cemetery listings for the state of California (1930s)
- Clipping file and indexed periodicals for local Catholic high schools, St. Mary's College (Moraga), and the College of Holy Names
- Extensive listing of specific names for local biographical research

CALIFORNIA STATE LIBRARY

California Section
P.O. Box 942837
Sacramento, CA 94237–0001

COLLECTION INCLUDES:

- Catholic newspapers from many of the Catholic dioceses within the state

SUTRO LIBRARY

Branch of the California State Library
480 Winston Drive
San Francisco, CA 94132

COLLECTION INCLUDES:

- D.A.R. cemetery inscriptions for the state of California
- Gray Mortuary records (San Francisco, 1850s)—includes many Catholic burials

SANTA CLARA UNIVERSITY/LIBRARY

Santa Clara, CA 95053

COLLECTION INCLUDES:

- Microfilm of early baptisms (1800s) for St. Joseph's Church and St. Patrick's Church (both Santa Clara)

CALIFORNIA STATE GENEALOGICAL SOCIETY

P.O. Box 77105
San Francisco, CA 94107

COLLECTION INCLUDES:

- Microfilm of J.C. O'Conner's mortuary and account records. This mortuary was used largely, although not exclusively, by Catholic families in San Francisco. The records cover the following dates: 1882–1896, 1898–1915, 1915–1919; account records: 1907–1919

SAN LUIS OBISPO COUNTY GENEALOGICAL SOCIETY

P.O. Box 4
Atascadero, CA 93423–0004

COLLECTION INCLUDES:

- Cemetery transcriptions for San Luis Obispo, including Catholic cemeteries (not in published form)

COLORADO

ARCHDIOCESE OF DENVER

1300 South Steele St.
Denver, CO 80210–2599
Telephone: (303) 722–4687

ARCHIVIST:
Sr. Mary Hughes

AREA INCLUDED IN ARCHDIOCESE:
Adams, Arapahoe, Boulder, Clear Creek, Denver, Eagle, Garfield, Gilpin, Grand, Jackson, Jefferson, Larimer, Logan, Moffat, Morgan, Phillips, Pitkin, Rio Blanco, Routt, Sedgwick, Summit, Washington, Weld, and Yuma counties.

Sacramental records for the Archdiocese of Denver are maintained on microfilm at the Archives.

FEES:
None.

DIOCESAN HISTORY:
Colorado Catholicism can be ordered from University Press of Colorado, P.O. Box 849, Niwot, CO 80544, for $39.95 and $1.75 postage.

CATHOLIC NEWSPAPER:
The Denver Catholic Register
200 Josephine St.
Denver, CO 80206

Est. 1905. *The Register* is on microfilm at the diocesan archives, the Denver Public Library, the Colorado Historical Society, and the University of Colorado Library in Boulder. Microfilm copies of *Colorado Catholic* (1884 to 1899) are in the Denver Public Library. The paper may also be inspected at the newspaper offices by appointment.

DIOCESE OF COLORADO SPRINGS

29 West Kiowa
Colorado Springs, CO 80903
Telephone: (719) 636–2345

ARCHIVIST:
Sr. Joseph Marie Jacobsen, OSB

AREA INCLUDED IN DIOCESE:
Chaffee, Cheyenne, Douglas, Elbert, El Paso, Kit Carson, Lake, Lincoln, Park, and Teller counties.

The Diocese of Colorado Springs was part of the Archdiocese of Denver until 1984. Post-1984 sacramental records for the Diocese of Colorado Springs are maintained at the parish level. Pre-1984 records are on microfilm at the Archdiocese of Denver. Baptismal certificates are issued by the parish where the sacrament was performed.

FEES:
Determined by the parish.

DIOCESE OF PUEBLO

1001 North Grand Ave.
Pueblo, CO 81003
Telephone: (719) 544–9861

AREA INCLUDED IN DIOCESE:
Alamosa, Archuleta, Baca, Bent, Conejos, Costilla, Crowley, Custer, Delta, Dolores, Fremont, Gunnison, Hinsdale, Huerfano, Kiowa, La Plata, Las Animas, Mesa, Mineral, Montezuma, Mintrose, Otero, Ouray, Prowers, Pueblo, Rio Grande, Saguache, San Juan, and San Miguel counties in Southern Colorado.

With the exception of newspaper information, the Diocese of Pueblo did not supply information.

CATHOLIC NEWSPAPER:
The Chronicle of Catholic Life
1001 North Grand Ave.
Pueblo, CO 81003

Est. 1988. The Catholic press has been active in the area since the inception of the diocese in 1941. *The Chronicle* was preceded by *Catholic Crosswinds*. The papers are on file at the diocesan offices. They contain few obituaries—mainly of priests and other religious communities.

ADDITIONAL COLORADO RESOURCES:

DENVER PUBLIC LIBRARY

1357 Broadway
Denver, CO 80203

COLLECTION INCLUDES:

- Records of the Archdiocese of Santa Fe, including baptisms, marriages, burials, patentes (letters from early Franciscan superiors) and diligencias matrimoniales (pre-nuptial investigations) on microfilm
- Extractions and translations of the Santa Fe registers (Spanish and English)
- *Denver Catholic Register*, 1915, 1917, 1921, 1929, and 1937
- Microfilm of the *Denver Catholic Register* 1920–1937
- *Denver Catholic Register* historical index, 1913–1939
- Microfilm of *Colorado Catholic*, 1892–1898
- W.P. Horan (Irish Catholic Mortuary, Denver) burial records index, 1900–1956
- Colorado cemetery directory
- Index to Old Mt. Olivet Cemetery, also known as the Doyle Cemetery and Catholic Cemetery (Chaffee Co.)
- "Who's Where in Leadville's Catholic Cemeteries" 1888–1981; an alphabetical listing of those interred in Mount Holy Cross, and St. Joseph's, Granite and Twin Lakes Cemeteries
- Lake County Cemeteries
- St. Mary Cemetery, Walsenburg, Huerfano Co.
- Fairmont Cemetery, (Denver), burial records, 1891–1990
- Germans from Russia file
- Statewide marriage index, 1900–1939
- Statewide marriage index, 1975–1990
- Statewide divorce index, 1900–1939
- Statewide divorce index, 1975–1990
- Denver Post divorce index, 1939–present

- Rocky Mountain News, 1944–present
- Materials of St. Rose of Lima Church and School, Denver
- Hispanic genealogy guides

PUEBLO LIBRARY DISTRICT

100 E. Abriendo Ave.
Pueblo, CO 81004

COLLECTION INCLUDES:

- *Catholic Crosswinds* and *The Chronicle* plus local papers 1868–present
- Local cemeteries collection
- Pueblo Catholic High School Book yearbooks (not complete)

COLORADO HISTORICAL SOCIETY

c/o The Colorado History Museum
1300 Broadway
Denver, CO 80203–2137

COLLECTION INCLUDES:

- *Denver Catholic Register*, 1906–1990, on microfilm
- *Colorado Catholicism*, a history of the Catholic Church in Colorado

The Colorado Historical Society will do research on a fee-for-search basis for those unable to visit the library.

HISTORICAL COLLECTIONS & ARCHIVES

Campus Box 184
University of Colorado
Boulder, CO 80309

COLLECTION INCLUDES:

- Microfilm of the *Denver Catholic Register*
- Cemetery transcriptions for Boulder and Weld counties

ARCHDIOCESE OF HARTFORD

Archives Office
134 Farmington Ave.
Hartford, CT 06105–3784
Telephone: (860) 541–6491

AREA INCLUDED IN DIOCESE:
Hartford, Litchfield, and New Haven counties.

The archdiocese has an open access policy and works readily with genealogical societies. Microfilms of sacramental registers are released in accordance with the census regulations. Researchers must write or telephone for an appointment, read the access policy, and abide by copyright laws. All baptismal records are kept at the local parishes; they are forwarded to the archives on request.

FEES:
Copying fee of 25 cents per page at the archives.

CATHOLIC NEWSPAPER:
The Catholic Transcript
785 Asylum Ave.
Hartford, CT 06105

Catholic journalism began in Connecticut in 1829. In 1873 the *Connecticut Catholic* was established. Two years later the name was changed to *The Catholic Transcript*. Copies may be viewed at the Hartford Public Library and at the newspaper offices by appointment.

DIOCESE OF BRIDGEPORT

Catholic Center
238 Jewett Ave.
Bridgeport, CT 06606
Telephone: (203) 372–4301

ARCHIVIST:
Rev. Msgr. John V. Horgan

AREA INCLUDED IN DIOCESE:
Fairfield County.

Sacramental records for the Diocese of Bridgeport are maintained at the parish level. Requests should be directed to the parish, if known. The Bishop Room at the Bridgeport Library has interesting items for researchers on Catholicism in the area, for example, clipping files and some parish histories.

FEES:
None.

DIOCESE OF NORWICH

201 Broadway
P.O. Box 587
Norwich, CT 06360
Telephone: (860) 887–9294

ARCHIVIST:
Rev. Ralph Kelley

AREA INCLUDED IN DIOCESE:
The counties of Middlesex, New London, Tolland, and Windham in the state of Connecticut and Fishers Island in the state of New York.

The diocese is not organized for genealogical research. Sacramental records are stored at the parishes, and requests should be addressed to the parish, if known. We can usually be of help in determining a parish for a known address.

FEES:
Determined by the parish.

DIOCESAN HISTORY:
Catholics of Eastern Connecticut: The Diocese of Norwich (1985) by Rev. Ralph Kelley.

DELAWARE

DIOCESE OF WILMINGTON

10 Monchanin Road
P.O. Box 4019
Wilmington, DE 19807
Telephone: (302) 655–0597

ARCHIVIST:
Donn Devine

AREA INCLUDED IN DIOCESE:
The entire state of Delaware and the following counties in the state of Maryland: Caroline, Cecil, Dorchester, Kent, Queen Anne's, Somerset, Talbot, Wicomico, and Worcester.

The Diocese of Wilmington Archives maintains reference microfilms of sacramental records through 1960. Original records are housed at the parishes where the sacraments were performed. Sacramental records for the diocese (registers, 1750–1960) were also recently microfilmed by the Genealogical Society of Utah and are available to researchers at the following locations: LDS Family History Library and Centers, Maryland Historical Society, (unrestricted records only); Historical Society of Delaware, Wilmington; Delaware Hall of Records, Dover; and the Maryland Hall of Records, Annapolis. The latter three will have forms for requesting the use of post-1920 baptisms. No restrictions apply to records of first communion, confirmation, marriage, death, or burial. Access to baptisms coincides with access to federal census enumerations, which are currently opened to public access after seventy-two years. Researchers may obtain special permission to view and copy their own family records on microfilm more recent than the latest open census by requesting written approval from the pastor of the parish in question, or, if the church has closed, from the current custodian of the records (usually the pastor of an adjoining parish or the diocesan archivist). The diocese operates two cemeteries in the Wilmington area: Cathedral, established in 1876; and All Saints, established in 1957.

FEES:
The customary donation for certificates is $5.00. Baptismal certificates are issued at the parish where the sacrament was performed.

CATHOLIC NEWSPAPER:
The Dialog
1925 Delaware Ave.
Wilmington, DE 19806

Est. 1965. On file at the diocesan archives.

ADDITIONAL DELAWARE RESOURCES:

DELAWARE STATE ARCHIVES

Hall of Records
Dover, DE 19901

COLLECTION INCLUDES:
- Tatnall Tombstone Collection—includes Catholic cemeteries
- *The Churches of Delaware*, by Frank R. Zebley, includes a short history of each church
- Sacramental records for Wilmington, 1796–1834; New Castle, 1845–1941; Dover, 1870–1945; Bohemia, (MD), 1790–1914; and Talbot County, (MD), 1803–1840

OLD BOHEMIA HISTORICAL SOCIETY

P.O. Box 61
Warwick, MD 21912

Society for oldest parish in the Diocese of Wilmington (St. Francis Xavier; now St. Joseph, Middletown, Delaware)

FLORIDA

ARCHDIOCESE OF MIAMI
9401 Biscayne Blvd.
Miami, FL 33138
Telephone: (305) 757–6241

AREA INCLUDED IN DIOCESE:
Broward, Dade and Monroe counties in southern Florida.

FEES:
$5.00 to $10.00, depending on the time required.

DIOCESE OF ORLANDO
421 E. Robinson
P.O. Box 1800
Orlando, FL 32802–1800
Telephone: (407) 246–4800

ARCHIVIST:
Ms. Jane Quinn

AREA INCLUDED IN DIOCESE:
Brevard, Lake, Marion, Orange, Osceola, Polk, Seminole, Sumter, and Volusia counties.

Genealogists (professional or amateur) should start their search for information at the parish level. The archives is not open to the public and is not staffed to do research for individuals.

FEES:
Determined by the parish.

DIOCESE OF PALM BEACH
9995 North Military Trail
Palm Beach Gardens, FL 33410
Telephone: (561) 775–9500

AREA INCLUDED IN DIOCESE:
Indian River, Martin, Okeechobee, Palm Beach, and St. Lucie counties.

Sacramental records are maintained at the parish level.

Fees:
Determined by the parish.

DIOCESE OF PENSACOLA– TALLAHASSEE
11 North "B" St.
Pensacola, FL 32501

Mailing address:
P.O. Drawer 17329
Pensacola, FL 32522
Telephone: (850) 432–1515

AREA INCLUDED IN DIOCESE:
Bay, Calhoun, Escambia, Franklin, Gadsden, Gulf, Holmes, Jackson, Jefferson, Leon, Liberty, Madison, Okaloosa, Santa Rosa, Taylor, Wakulla, Walton, and Washington counties.

All sacramental records are maintained at the parish level, where certificates are issued.

FEES:
None

DIOCESE OF ST. AUGUSTINE
11625 Old St. Augustine Rd.
Jacksonville, FL 32258

Mailing address:
P.O. Box 24000
Jacksonville, FL 32241–4000
Telephone: (904) 262–3200

AREA INCLUDED IN DIOCESE:
Alachua, Baker, Bradford, Clay, Columbia, Dixie, Duval, Flagler, Gilchrist, Hamilton, Lafayette, Levy, Nassau, Putnam, St. Johns, Suwanee, and Union counties in northeastern Florida.

Archives of the Diocese of St. Augustine maintain the original Cathedral Basilica Parish Registers of the St. Augustine diocese. The earliest entry is dated 25 June 1594 and begins the oldest written records of American origin in the United States. An adjunct to the St. Augustine Cathedral's oldest records is a one-volume parish register that was begun by a Minorcan priest missionary to Catholics in New Smyrna Beach. His records began in 1768 and continued there until the Minorcans resettled in St. Augustine in 1777. Copies of the sacramental records of the Diocese of St. Augustine are available to researchers at the St. Augustine Historical Society, 271 Charlotte Street, St. Augustine, FL, 32084, telephone: (904) 824–2872. The society library is open to the public.

Records housed at the society library are as follows:

Baptisms:	Marriages:	Deaths:
1594–1763	1594–1756	1623–1638
1768–1971	1776–1945	1720–1763
		1784–1974

Pardos-Morenos-Indios: 1736–1763 (sacramental records for African Americans, Indians, and those of mixed races—separated by color.)

All of the records are on microfilm or are photostat copies. There is also an abstracted index of the records. For those unable to visit the library, written requests are accepted. For simple requests that include accurate information, so that the record can be retrieved easily, the fees are as stated below for copies; the researcher will be billed. If research needs to be done at the library, the fee is $10.00 per hour. The society library also includes a large collection of Florida genealogies, many of which are donated to the library as research on Florida families is completed.

FEES:
$1.00 per microfilm page; 25 cents per photocopy page; research in the library costs $10.00 per hour.

DIOCESE OF ST. PETERSBURG
P.O. Box 40200
St. Petersburg, FL 33743
Telephone: (813) 344–1611

AREA INCLUDED IN DIOCESE:
Citrus, Hernando, Hillsborough, Pasco, and Pinellas counties.

Sacramental records are maintained at the parish level.

Fees:
None.

DIOCESE OF VENICE
1000 Pinebrook Ave.
Venice, FL 34292

Mailing:
P.O. Box 2006
Venice, FL 34284
Telephone: (941) 484–9543

AREA INCLUDED IN DIOCESE:
Charlotte, Collier, DeSoto, Glades, Hardee, Hendry, Highlands, Lee, Manatee, and Sarasota counties.

Sacramental records are maintained at the parish level.

FEES:
Decided at the parish.

ADDITIONAL FLORIDA RESOURCES:

STATE LIBRARY OF FLORIDA

R.A. Gray Building
Tallahassee, FL 32301

COLLECTION INCLUDES:
- Microfilm of *Florida Catholic*, 1946–1951

P.K. YONGE LIBRARY OF FLORIDA HISTORY

University of Florida
Gainesville, FL 32601

COLLECTION INCLUDES:
- Microfilm of *Florida Catholic* (Orlando), 1939–present

GEORGIA

ARCHDIOCESE OF ATLANTA

680 West Peachtree St. N.W.
Atlanta, GA 30308–1884
Telephone: (404) 888–7801

ARCHIVIST:
Mr. Anthony R. Dees

AREA INCLUDED IN DIOCESE:
Baldwin, Banks, Barrow, Bartow, Butts, Carroll, Catoosa, Chattooga, Cherokee, Clarke, Clayton, Cobb, Coweta, Dade, Dawson, DeKalb, Douglas, Elbert, Fannin, Fayette, Floyd, Forsyth, Franklin, Fulton, Gilmer, Gordon, Greene, Gwinnett, Habersham, Hall, Hancock, Haralson, Hart, Heard, Henry, Jackson, Jasper, Lamar, Lincoln, Lumpkin, Madison, McDuffie, Meriwether, Monroe, Morgan, Murray, Newton, Oconee, Oglethorpe, Paulding, Pickens, Pike, Polk, Putnam, Rabun, Rockdale, Spalding, Stephens, Taliaferro, Towns, Troup, Union, Upson, Walker, Walton, Warren, White, Whitfield, and Wilkes counties in northern Georgia.

Original sacramental records are stored at the parish level. For copies of certificates, consult with the parish. If the parish is in question, the archivist can often help to determine the parish if precise information is included in the inquiry. Generally requests are forwarded to the appropriate parish. Microfilm copies of records of the Church of Purification at Sharon (formerly Locust Grove) for 1822–1845 are at the Georgia Department of Archives and History.

FEES:
Decided at the parish.

CATHOLIC NEWSPAPER:
The Georgia Bulletin
680 West Peachtree St. N.W.
Atlanta, GA 30308–1984

Est. 1963. Microfilm of *The Georgia Bulletin* and earlier Georgia newspapers are housed at the University of Georgia Library in Athens and at any library that subscribes to the Georgia Newspaper Project of university's microfilm service. Microfilm may also be researched on a limited basis at the newspaper office by appointment.

DIOCESE OF SAVANNAH

Catholic Pastoral Center
601 East Liberty St.
Savannah, GA 31401–5196
Telephone: (912) 238–2320

AREA INCLUDED IN DIOCESE:
Appling, Atkinson, Bacon, Baker, Ben Hill, Berrien, Bibb, Bleckley, Brantley, Brooks, Bryan, Bulloch, Burke, Calhoun, Camden, Candler, Charlton, Chatham, Chattahoochee, Clay, Clinch, Coffee, Colquitt, Columbia, Cook, Crawford, Crisp, Decatur, Dodge, Dooly, Dougherty, Early, Echols, Effingham, Glynn, Grady, Harris, Houston, Irwin, Jeff Davis, Jefferson, Jenkins, Johnson, Jones, Lanier, Laurens, Lee, Liberty, Long, Lowndes, Macon, Marion, McIntosh, Miller, Mitchell, Montgomery, Muscogee, Peach, Pierce, Pulaski, Quitman, Randolph, Richmond, Schley, Screven, Seminole, Stewart, Sumter, Talbot, Tattnall, Taylor, Telfair, Terrell, Thomas, Tift, Toombs, Treutlen, Turner, Twiggs, Ware, Washington, Wayne, Webster, Wheeler, Wilcox, Wilkinson, and Worth counties in southern Georgia.

Early records for the Diocese of Savannah are located at the Pastoral Center. The diocese maintains one cemetery in Savannah; records are kept at the Pastoral Center.

FEES:
Donations appreciated.

CATHOLIC NEWSPAPER:

The Southern Cross
601 E. 6th St.
Waynesboro, GA 30830

Est. 1963. An earlier paper, *The Bulletin of the Catholic Laymen's Association of Georgia*, was published from 1920 through 1962. Some microfilm and all bound volumes are housed at the diocesan archives. Some years of *The Southern Cross* are also located at the University of Georgia Library in Athens.

ADDITIONAL GEORGIA RESOURCES:

THE AUGUSTA GENEALOGICAL SOCIETY

P.O. Box 3743
Augusta, GA 30914–3743

COLLECTION INCLUDES:

- Around 5,000 volumes, many of them family records, for Georgia and South Carolina.
- Augusta had a very large Irish population in the nineteenth century; the society has publications available for purchase which should be an excellent source for those with Irish Catholic ancestors in the Augusta area:
- *Irish Nativities in Magnolia Cemetery, Augusta, Georgia*. 180 pages, hard cover, acid free paper; $35.00. Contains exact tombstone inscriptions of stones showing an Irish nativity—mostly from immigrants of mid-1800s. Part II has sextons' records of all Irish burials showing Ireland as nativity, from 1870 to 1900.
- *Ancestoring—Journal of Augusta Genealogical Society*, vol. 13, contains: "18th Century Catholic Mission in Augusta for French Refugees and Irish Immigrants" and "Augusta's Roman Catholic Church of the Most Holy Trinity, Book One, 1810-1824" (baptisms and marriages). Illustrated, marriage bond facsimile. Soft cover, $6.50

These publications are available from the Augusta Genealogical Society. Please include $2.00 postage and handling for hardback, $1.00 for soft cover.

HAWAII

DIOCESE OF HONOLULU

1184 Bishop Street
Honolulu, HI 96813
Telephone: (808) 533–1791

ARCHIVIST:
Rev. Louis Yim

AREA INCLUDED IN DIOCESE:
The Hawaiian Islands and the Equatorial, Palmyra, Washington, Fanning, and Christmas Islands.

Sacramental records for the Diocese of Honolulu are maintained at the parish level. Requests for information or certificates should be made directly to the parish where the sacrament was performed. If the parish is not known, requests may be directed to the Chancery office. It is recommended that research be complete before requesting records. Necessary information includes the full name of the individual that you wish researched, approximate dates, address of the individual at the time the sacrament would have been administered (sometimes the neighborhood can be helpful if the address is unknown), and the type of record you wish searched.

FEES:
$5.00 is the suggested donation for research time.

CATHOLIC NEWSPAPER:

Hawaii Catholic Herald
1184 Bishop Street
Honolulu, HI 96813

Est. 1936. Preceded by *The Church Bells,* 1926-1935. Most years of the paper are available at the Hamilton Library, University of Hawaii. The papers may also be inspected at the newspaper offices by appointment.

ADDITIONAL HAWAII RESOURCES:

HAWAII STATE PUBLIC LIBRARY

478 S. King Street
Honolulu, HI 96813

COLLECTION INCLUDES:
• Large collection of U.S. mainland materials
• Microfilm of *Hawaii Catholic Herald* from 1970
• Index to obituaries published in Hawaii newspapers; 1836–1950
• Yearbooks from St. Louis High School (29 years; earliest is 1935)
• Yearbooks from St. Francis Convent (30 years; earliest is 1948)
• Yearbooks from St. Joseph School on Hilo (18 years; earliest is 1952)

DIOCESE OF BOISE

303 Federal Way
P.O. Box 769
Boise, ID 83701–0769
Telephone: (208) 342–1311

AREA INCLUDED IN DIOCESE:

The entire state of Idaho.

Records located in the Chancery are minimal except in the area of sacraments. Early sacramental records for the state have also been released to the Idaho State Historical Society.

FEES:

None for single copies. Large requests are charged a nominal fee and postage.

ADDITIONAL IDAHO RESOURCES:

IDAHO STATE HISTORICAL SOCIETY

Library and Archives and Genealogy Libraries
450 North 4th
Boise, ID 83702

COLLECTION INCLUDES:

• The Idaho State Historical Society is in the process of indexing the Diocese of Boise's sacramental records.
• The collection also includes gravestone transcriptions from Morris Hill Cemetery.

ARCHDIOCESE OF CHICAGO

155 East Superior
Chicago, IL 60611
Telephone: (312) 751–8150

AREA INCLUDED IN DIOCESE:
Cook and Lake counties.

Direct requests for records to the parish where the sacrament was performed. The Archives and Records Center of the Archdiocese of Chicago (5150 Northwest Highway, Chicago, IL, 60630) maintains microfilmed copies of parish registers and original records of closed parishes. The center's research policy stipulate that "genealogical and sacramental records research must be carried on by mail."

The Genealogical Society of Utah has microfilmed the pre-1915 sacramental records of all churches in the archdiocese. These are available for viewing at the Family History Library in Salt Lake City and through its family history centers. The archives has the records of some closed parishes. If seeking records from an open parish, contact the parish directly.

Locations of Roman Catholic Churches, 1850–1900, by Jack Bochar (Geneva, Ill: the author, 1990) is a map guide with alphabetical, chronological, and ethnic composition listings of 331 churches in the Archdiocese of Chicago. It includes an addendum with Family History Library microfilm numbers for the individual parishes.

FEES:
Synopses of pre-1915 sacramental records are available free of charge, but donations are accepted. Actual certificates stamped "for genealogical purposes" cost $5.00 per certificate.

DIOCESAN HISTORY:
Catholicism Chicago Style (1993) by Ellen Skerrett, et al.

A History of the Parishes of the Archdiocese of Chicago (1980) by Rev. Msgr. Harry C. Koenig, STD (editor).

Diamond Jubilee of the Archdiocese of Chicago (1920).

DIOCESE OF BELLEVILLE

Archives
222 South Third St.
Belleville, IL 62220

AREA INCLUDED IN DIOCESE:
Alexander, Clay, Clinton, Edwards, Franklin, Gallatin, Hamilton, Hardin, Jackson, Jefferson, Johnson, Lawrence, Marion, Massac, Monroe, Perry, Pope, Pulaski, Randolph, Richland, Saline, St. Claire, Union, Wabash, Washington, Wayne, White, and Williamson counties.

Genealogists should start searching in the appropriate parish, not at the archives. The archives retains sacramental records for those parishes in the diocese that have been closed.

FEES:
Determined by the parish.

DIOCESE OF JOLIET

Chancery
425 Summit St.
Joliet, IL 60435–7193
Telephone: (815) 722–6606

AREA INCLUDED IN DIOCESE:
DuPage, Ford, Grundy, Iroquois, Kankakee, Kendall, and Will counties.

Sacramental records for the diocese are retained at the parish level. Requests for information or certificates should be directed to the parish of origin. When the parish is unknown, the diocese can often be of help if sufficient information is provided.

FEES:
None

CATHOLIC NEWSPAPER:
The New Catholic Explorer
402 S. Independence Blvd.
Romeoville, IL 60441

Est. 1965. Established as the *Joliet Catholic Explorer*.
Bound volumes are located at the newspaper offices.

DIOCESE OF PEORIA

Chancery Office
607 N.E. Madison Ave.
P.O. Box 1406
Peoria, IL 61655
Telephone: (309) 671–1550

AREA INCLUDED IN DIOCESE:
Bureau, Champaign, DeWitt, Fulton, Hancock,
Henderson, Henry, Knox, LaSalle, Livingston,
Logan, Marshall, Mason, McDonough, McLean,
Mercer, Peoria, Piatt, Putnam, Rock Island,
Schuyler, Stark, Tazewell, Vermilion, Warren, and
Woodford counties.

Most of the sacramental records are maintained at
the parish level. Contact the parish of origin, if
known. The diocese can often help in determining a
parish if sufficient information is provided.

FEES:
None, unless a request is unusually time consuming.

CATHOLIC NEWSPAPER:
The Catholic Post
P.O. Box 1722
Peoria, IL 61656

Est. 1934. Microfilm and bound volumes are housed
at *The Post* offices and may be researched there by
appointment.

DIOCESE OF ROCKFORD

1245 N. Court St.
Rockford, IL 61103–6290
Telephone: (815) 962–3709

AREA INCLUDED IN DIOCESE:
Boone, Carroll, De Kalb, Jo Daviess, Kane, Lee,
McHenry, Ogle, Stephenson, Whiteside, and
Winnebago counties.

Inquiries are best addressed to the appropriate
parish, if known. The diocese has microfilm copies
of records that currently are held by the individual
parishes. Records of parishes established in the
nineteenth century and subsequently closed are
sometimes found in the closest existing parish.
Records can be accessed only if the parish and date
are known prior to inquiry. The Diocese of
Rockford was established in 1908 when twelve (now
eleven) counties were detached from the
Archdiocese of Chicago. Record transfers prior to
that time are often vague when current searches are
made.

FEES:
Determined by the parish.

CATHOLIC NEWSPAPER:
The Observer
921 W. State St.
Rockford, IL 61102

Est. 1935. Papers may be researched on site by
appointment.

DIOCESE OF SPRINGFIELD IN ILLINOIS

Catholic Pastoral Center
1615 West Washington
P.O. Box 3187
Springfield, IL 62708–3187
Telephone: (217) 698–8500

AREA INCLUDED IN DIOCESE:

Adams, Bond, Brown, Calhoun, Cass, Christian, Clark, Coles, Crawford, Cumberland, Douglas, Edgar, Effingham, Fayette, Greene, Jasper, Jersey, Macon, Macoupin, Madison, Menard, Montgomery, Morgan, Moultrie, Pike, Sangamon, Scott, and Shelby counties.

All sacramental records are kept in the parishes where the sacrament was administered.

FEES:

Determined by the parish.

CATHOLIC NEWSPAPER:

The Catholic Times
514 East Lawrence St.
Springfield, IL 62703

Est. 1896. Earlier names of this paper were *Western Catholic* and *Time and Eternity*. Microfilms are located at the Illinois State Historical Society, Old State Capitol, Springfield, IL, 62701–1507. Microfilms date from 17 October 1908 to 22 December 1991.

ADDITIONAL ILLINOIS RESOURCES:

SOUTH SUBURBAN GENEALOGICAL & HISTORICAL SOCIETY

P.O. Box 96
South Holland, IL 60473

COLLECTION INCLUDES:

• The SSGHS has done extensive research in the South Suburban area, including cemeteries, churches, funeral home records, schools, etc. Much of the material has been published in *Where the Trails Cross*, the SSGHS quarterly. For information, contact the SSGHS at the above address.

INDIANA

ARCHDIOCESE OF INDIANAPOLIS
1400 N. Meridian St.
P.O. Box 1410
Indianapolis, IN 46206
Telephone: (317) 236–1400

ARCHIVIST:
Rev. Michael Widner

AREA INCLUDED IN DIOCESE:
Bartholomew, Brown, Clark, Clay, Crawford, Dearborn, Decatur, Fayette, Floyd, Franklin, Hancock, Harrison, Hendricks, Henry, Jackson, Jefferson, Jennings, Johnson, Lawrence, Marion, Monroe, Morgan, Ohio, Orange, Owen, Parke, Perry, Putnam, Ripley, Rush, Scott, Shelby, Switzerland, Union, Vermillion, Vigo, Washington, Wayne counties and the township of Harrison in Spencer County.

Sacramental records for the Archdiocese of Indianapolis were microfilmed by the Genealogical Society of Utah in 1988 (through 1917). They are available for researchers at the LDS Family History Library in Salt Lake City and through its family history centers, the Indiana Historical Society, and at the Archdiocesan Archives. Baptismal certificates are not issued at the archives, but it will issue abstracts or written copies.

FEES:
None.

DIOCESAN HISTORY:
The Catholic Church in Indiana 1686-1814 (1976) by Msgr. John J. Doyle.

The Catholic Church in the Diocese of Vincennes 1847-77 (1946) by Sr. Mary Carol Schroeder, OSF.

The Catholic Church in Indiana 1793-1834 (1940) by Rev. Thomas McAvoy, CSC.

History of the Catholic Church in Indiana (1898) by Col. Charles Blanchard (editor).

History of the Catholic Church in the Diocese of Vincennes (1883) by Rev. Herman J. Aldering.

DIOCESE OF EVANSVILLE
4200 N. Kentucky Ave.
P.O. Box 4169
Evansville, IN 47724–0169
Telephone: (812) 424–5536

AREA INCLUDED IN DIOCESE:
Daviess, Dubois, Gibson, Greene, Knox, Martin, Pike, Posey, Spencer (except the township of Harrison), Sullivan, Vanderburgh, and Warrick counties.

The diocese is not staffed to do research for genealogical purposes. Sacramental records for the diocese have been microfilmed by the Genealogical Society of Utah. They are available to researchers through the LDS Family History Library in Salt Lake City and its family history centers. Copies of baptismal records must be obtained at the parish level.

FEES:
Determined by the parish.

DIOCESE OF FORT WAYNE–SOUTH BEND
1103 South Calhoun St.
P.O. Box 390
Fort Wayne, IN 46801
Telephone: (219) 422–4611

AREA INCLUDED IN DIOCESE:
Adams, Allen, DeKalb, Elkhart, Huntington, Kosciusko, Lagrange, Marshall, Noble, St. Joseph, Steuben, Wabash, Wells, and Whitley counties.

The Genealogical Society of Utah has microfilmed the diocese's records through 1910. They are available for researchers at the LDS Family History Library in Salt Lake City and its family history centers, the Fort Wayne Public Library, and the Indiana State Library. Baptismal certificates must be obtained through the parish where the sacrament was performed.

FEES:
Determined by the parish.

DIOCESE OF GARY

9292 Broadway
Merrillville, IN 46410
Telephone: (219) 769–9292

AREA INCLUDED IN DIOCESE:
Lake, LaPorte, Porter, and Starke counties.

Sacramental records for the diocese are maintained at the parish level. Requests should be directed to the parish, if known. The records have also been microfilmed by the Genealogical Society of Utah and are available at the Family History Library in Salt Lake City and its family history centers.

FEES:
None.

DIOCESE OF LAFAYETTE

P.O. Box 260
Lafayette, IN 47902–0260
Telephone: (765) 742–0275

AREA INCLUDED IN DIOCESE:
Benton, Blackford, Boone, Carroll, Cass, Clinton, Delaware, Fountain, Fulton, Grant, Hamilton, Howard, Jasper, Jay, Madison, Miami, Montgomery, Newton, Pulaski, Randolph, Tippecanoe, Tipton, Warren, and White counties.

Sacramental records are maintained at the parish level. Requests should be directed to the parish in question, if known. The chancery can often be of help in determining a parish if precise information is provided. Records have also been microfilmed by the Genealogical Society of Utah and are available at the LDS Family History Library in Salt Lake City and its family history centers.

FEES:
None

CATHOLIC NEWSPAPER:
The Sunday Visitor
P.O. Box 1603
Lafayette, IN 47902

Est. 1945. Papers may be researched at the newspaper offices, by appointment. Not indexed.

IOWA

ARCHDIOCESE OF DUBUQUE

1229 Mt. Loretta Ave.
P.O. Box 479
Dubuque, IA 52004–0479
Telephone: (319) 556–2580

ARCHIVIST:
Msgr. Edgar Kurt

Allamakee, Benton, Black Hawk, Bremer, Buchanan, Butler, Cerro Gordo, Chickasaw, Clayton, Delaware, Dubuque, Fayette, Floyd, Franklin, Grundy, Hamilton, Hancock, Hardin, Howard, Jackson, Jones, Linn, Marshall, Mitchell, Story, Winnebago, Winneshiek, Worth, and Wright countries.

All sacramental and death records for the diocese are stored at the parish level. Requests should be sent to the parish involved, if known. The archives is in the process of filing burial registrations from the parishes and cemeteries, beginning with the 1937 documents. Where a priest is pastor of more than one parish and/or an oratory, the records for all places are in the parish of residence. Most of the religious communities that have worked and taught in the archdiocese also have efficient archives.

FEES:
Determined by the parish. Some pastors refuse to look up records for other than sacramental purposes.

CATHOLIC NEWSPAPER:
The Witness
P.O. Box 917
Dubuque, IA 52004

Est. 1921. Microfilms of the paper are housed at Loras College Library, 1450 Alta Vista St., Dubuque, IA 52001. Bound volumes of the paper may be researched at *The Witness* offices by appointment.

DIOCESE OF DAVENPORT

St. Vincent Center
2706 N. Gaines St.
Davenport, IA 52804
Telephone: (319) 324–1911

ARCHIVIST:
Sr. Madeleine Marie Schmidt, CHM

AREA INCLUDED IN DIOCESE:
Appanoose, Cedar, Clinton, Davis, Des Moines, Henry, Iowa, Jasper, Jefferson, Johnson, Keokuk, Lee, Louisa, Mahaska, Marion, Monroe, Muscatine, Poweshiek, Scott, Van Buren, Wapello, and Washington counties.

Sacramental records prior to 1918 are in the parishes where the sacraments were given. Microfilmed records created since 1918 are not open for public use, however, some confirmation of records can be furnished to qualified related persons.

FEES:
Determined by the parish.

DIOCESAN HISTORY:
Seasons of Growth: A History of the Diocese of Davenport, 1881-1981 (1981), by Sister Madeleine Marie Schmidt, CHM, can be ordered in hardcover $12.00 or softcover for $6.00 and postage.

CATHOLIC NEWSPAPER:
The Catholic Messenger
P.O. Box 460
103 East 2nd St.
Davenport, IA 52805

Est. 1883. Microfilms are in the library of St. Ambrose University in Davenport, also at the Davenport Public Library from about 1944.

DIOCESE OF DES MOINES

601 Grand Ave.
P.O. Box 1816
Des Moines, IA 50306
Telephone: (515) 243-7653

ARCHIVIST:
Fr. Paul Bianchi

AREA INCLUDED IN DIOCESE:
Adair, Adams, Audubon, Cass, Clarke, Dallas, Decatur, Fremont, Guthrie, Harrison, Lucas, Madison, Mills, Montgomery, Page, Polk, Pottawattamie, Ringgold, Shelby, Taylor, Union, Warren, and Wayne counties.

Records of historical significance are kept at the chancery. Requests for documents and other items related to genealogical research are received on a fairly regular basis. Emphasis is given to requests for verification of sacramental records and other data that is needed for church requirements. Contact the parish directly, if known.

FEES:
None

CATHOLIC NEWSPAPER:
The Catholic Mirror
818 5th Ave.
P.O. Box 10372
Des Moines, IA 50306

Est. 1936. Preceded by *The Catholic Messenger* established in 1883. Copies of *The Mirror* may be researched by appointment at the newspaper offices.

DIOCESE OF SIOUX CITY

1821 Jackson St.
P.O. Box 3379
Sioux City, IA 51102
Telephone: (712) 255-7933

ARCHIVIST:
Sr. Kevin Cummings, PBVM

AREA INCLUDED IN DIOCESE:
Boone, Buena Vista, Calhoun, Carroll, Cherokee, Clay, Crawford, Dickinson, Emmet, Greene, Humboldt, Ida, Kossuth, Lyon, Monona, O'Brien, Osceola, Palo Alto, Plymouth, Pocahontas, Sac, Sioux, Webster, and Woodbury counties.

Sacramental records for the Diocese of Sioux City are maintained in the parishes in which the sacrament was given. Although the diocese was established in 1902, records predate the diocese by several years. In the early days, the priests from Fort Dodge ranged far and wide in their work, so there are records from as far away as Emmetsburg. (The first Baptism in Emmetsburg was performed on 24 January 1872.) Other baptisms performed during the early days are recorded in Algona, Sheldon, and "most of the territory around here." There are notes on early days in Algona and St. Joseph (Bode). The archives also holds transcripts of cathedral and Breda baptisms and, in the case of Breda, a census an early priest took in which he indicated place of origin, etc. The archivist can usually indicate which parish has baptismal information on an individual when necessary information is given (date, location, and names).

FEES:
Donations are appreciated for research performed.

ADDITIONAL IOWA RESOURCES:

STATE HISTORICAL SOCIETY OF IOWA

402 Iowa Ave.
Iowa City, IA 52240-1806

COLLECTION INCLUDES:
• Cemetery listings—arranged by county
• Local church histories
• Histories and directories of the Iowa dioceses and some of the prominent clergy in the state

NORTH CENTRAL IOWA GENEALOGICAL SOCIETY

P.O. Box 237
Mason City, IA 50401

The North Central Iowa Genealogical Society has access to all early Catholic burial and cemetery records and church records, 1870s–1900s for Mason City.

BUENA VISTA COUNTY GENEALOGICAL SOCIETY

609 Erie St.
Storm Lake, IA 50588

COLLECTION INCLUDES:
- Transcripts of St. Mary's Catholic Cemetery (located east of Storm Lake)
- Transcripts of Newell Catholic Cemetery (located northwest of Newell; no longer in use)
- Legible tombstones of both cemeteries have been read and fully transcribed and printed according to townships. The transcripts are available for purchase from the Buena Vista County Genealogical Society. Direct inquiries to the above address.

NORTH EAST IOWA GENEALOGICAL SOCIETY

c/o Grout Museum
503 South
Waterloo, IA 50701

COLLECTION INCLUDES:
- Histories of several local parishes
- Index to Calvary Cemetery (Waterloo)
- Future plans include indexing the Catholic Cemetery in Gilbertville

THE NORTHWEST IOWA GENEALOGICAL SOCIETY

46 First St. S.W.
Le Mars, IA 51031

COLLECTION INCLUDES:
- Index of all Catholic Cemeteries in Plymouth County. The society also has access to funeral home records and Catholic church records. Long range plans are to copy the Catholic funeral home records and the cemetery plot records.

KANSAS

ARCHDIOCESE OF KANSAS CITY IN KANSAS

Savior Pastoral Center
12615 Parallel Parkway
Kansas City, KS 66109
Telephone: (913) 721–1570

ARCHIVIST:
Rev. Leo Cooper

AREA INCLUDED IN DIOCESE:
Anderson, Atchison, Brown, Coffey, Doniphan, Douglas, Franklin, Jackson, Jefferson, Johnson, Leavenworth, Linn, Marshall, Miami, Nemaha, Osage, Pottawatomie, Shawnee, Wabaunsee, and Wyandotte counties.

Sacramental records for the archdiocese to 1958 are on microfilm in the archives. Also on microfilm in the archives are the Mt. Calvary Cemetery records (Leavenworth) and records from the Federal Penitentiary in Leavenworth. The Sisters of Charity, based in Leavenworth, and the Benedictine Sisters and Benedictine Abbey in Atchison have their own archives. A lot of material on the Indian Missions can be found in the Jesuit Provincial Archives in St. Louis.

FEES:
None

CATHOLIC NEWSPAPER:
The Leaven
12615 Parallel Parkway
Kansas City, KS 66109

Est. 1939. *The Eastern Kansas Register* and *The Leaven* are on microfilm at the archives, but at the present time there is no reader/printer available to researchers. Copies may also be found at the Kansas State Historical Society in Topeka and the Kansas City Public Library. Not indexed.

DIOCESE OF DODGE CITY

910 Central Ave.
P.O. Box 849
Dodge City, KS 67801
Telephone: (316) 227–1500

ARCHIVIST:
Tim Wenzl

AREA INCLUDED IN DIOCESE:
Barber, Barton, Clark, Comanche, Edwards, Finney, Ford, Grant, Gray, Greeley, Hamilton, Haskell, Hodgeman, Kearny, Kiowa, Lane, Meade, Morton, Ness, Pawnee, Pratt, Rush, Scott, Seward, Stafford, Stanton, Stevens, and Wichita counties.

Sacramental records for the Diocese are maintained at the parish level.

FEES:
Determined by the parish.

CATHOLIC NEWSPAPER:
Southwest Kansas Register
P.O. Box 1317
Dodge City, KS 67801

Est. 1951. Very few obituaries; probably of limited value to genealogists.

DIOCESE OF SALINA

P.O. Box 980
Salina, KS 67402–0980
Telephone: (913) 827–8746

ARCHIVIST:
Msgr. James Hake

AREA INCLUDED IN THE DIOCESE:
Cheyenne, Clay, Cloud, Decatur, Dickinson, Ellis, Ellsworth, Geary, Gove, Graham, Jewell, Lincoln, Logan, Mitchell, Norton, Osborne, Ottowa,

Phillips, Rawlins, Republic, Riley, Rooks, Russell, Saline, Sheridan, Sherman, Smith, Thomas, Trego, Wallace, and Washington counties.

Sacramental records for the early years of the diocese are maintained at the archives.

DIOCESAN HISTORY:
Harvest of Faith: A History of the Diocese of Salina (Dallas, Tex.: Taylor Publishing Co., 1987)

FEES:
None

CATHOLIC NEWSPAPER:
Northwestern Kansas Register
P.O. Box 1038
Salina, KS 67402

Est. 1937. On microfilm at the archives but not easily accessible at present. Papers may be researched at the newspaper offices.

DIOCESE OF WICHITA
424 North Broadway
Wichita, KS 67202
Telephone: (316) 269–3900

AREA INCLUDED IN DIOCESE:
Allen, Bourbon, Butler, Chase, Chautauqua, Cherokee, Cowley, Crawford, Elk, Greenwood, Harper, Harvey, Kingman, Labette, Marion, McPherson, Montgomery, Morris, Neosho, Reno, Rice, Sedgwick, Sumner, Wilson, and Woodson counties.

Sacramental records for the diocese are kept at the parish level. Records within the diocesan archives are very limited. Direct inquiries to the parish, if known.

FEES:
None

KENTUCKY

ARCHDIOCESE OF LOUISVILLE

212 East College St.
P.O. Box 1073
Louisville, KY 40201
Telephone: (502) 585–3291

AREA INCLUDED IN THE DIOCESE:

Adair, Barren, Bullitt, Casey, Clinton, Cumberland, Green, Hardin, Hart, Henry, Jefferson, Larue, Marion, Meade, Metcalfe, Monroe, Nelson, Oldham, Russell, Shelby, Spencer, Taylor, Trimble, and Washington counties.

Sacramental records for the Archdiocese of Louisville are found at the parish level, where certificates are issued. Requests should be directed to the parish, if known.

FEES:

Donations are appreciated.

DIOCESAN HISTORY:

An American Holy Land: A History of the Archiodese of Louisville (1987) by Clyde F. Crews.

CATHOLIC NEWSPAPER:

The Record
Maloney Center
1200 South Shelby St.
Louisville, KY 40203–2600

Est. 1878. Microfilms of the paper are housed at the University of Kentucky Library in Lexington, Bellarmine College in Louisville, and the main branch of the Louisville Public Library (not all years). Not indexed. Papers may also be inspected at the newspaper offices by appointment (not all years are available).

DIOCESE OF COVINGTON

The Catholic Center
P.O. Box 18548
Erlanger, KY 41018–0548
Telephone: (606) 283–6210

ARCHIVIST:

Sr. Mary Philip Trauth, SND

AREA INCLUDED IN DIOCESE:

Bracken, Boone, Campbell, Carroll, Fleming, Gallatin, Grant, Harrison, Kenton, Lewis, Mason, Owen, Pendleton, and Robertson counties.

Sacramental records for the diocese remain in the individual parishes, where certificates are issued. The Catholic Cemeteries Office is located at the Catholic Center. The diocesan cemeteries are St. John Cemetery, Ft. Mitchell; St. Joseph Cemetery, Wilder; St. Joseph Cemetery, Cold Spring; St. Mary Cemetery, Ft. Mitchell; St. Stephen Cemetery, Ft. Thomas; and Resurrection Cemetery, Union. There are also several parish cemeteries in the diocese. Contact the pastor of the parish.

FEES:

Determined by the parish.

DIOCESAN HISTORY:

History of the Diocese of Covington, Kentucky (1954) by Rev. Paul E. Ryan.

CATHOLIC NEWSPAPER:

The Messenger
P.O. Box 18068
Covington, KY 41018

Est. 1926. (At one time *The Sunday Visitor*.) The paper is on microfilm at the University of Kentucky Library in Lexington. Bound volumes are located at the newspaper office in Erlanger. Researchers are welcome. Not indexed.

DIOCESE OF LEXINGTON

The Catholic Center
P.O. Box 12350
1310 Leestown Road
Lexington, KY 40582–2350
Telephone: (606) 253–1993

ARCHIVIST:
Sr. Mary Kevan Seibert, SND

AREA INCLUDED IN DIOCESE:
Anderson, Bath, Bell, Bourbon, Boyd, Boyle, Breathitt, Carter, Clark, Clay, Elliott, Estill, Fayette, Floyd, Franklin, Garrard, Greenup, Harlan, Jackson, Jessamine, Johnson, Knott, Knox, Laurel, Lawrence, Lee, Leslie, Letcher, Lincoln, McCreary, Madison, Magoffin, Martin, Menifee, Mercer, Montgomery, Morgan, Nicholas, Owsley, Perry, Pike, Powell, Pulaski, Rockcastle, Rowan, Scott, Wayne, Whitley, Wolfe, and Woodford counties.

The Diocese of Lexington was created in 1988, taking seven counties from the Archdiocese of Louisville and forty-three counties from the Diocese of Covington. The Diocese of Covington has all records prior to 1988. Copies of sacramental records held in Lexington are from 1950 to the present.

DIOCESAN HISTORY:
History of the Diocese of Covington, Kentucky (1954) by Rev. Paul E. Ryan (includes the history of the Diocese of Lexington).

CATHOLIC NEWSPAPER:
Cross Roads
The Catholic Center
Lexington, KY 40582–2350

Est. 1988. Refer to Covington and Louisville papers—that area was part of those dioceses prior to 1988.

DIOCESE OF OWENSBORO

Catholic Pastoral Center
600 Locust Street
Owensboro, KY 42301
Telephone: (502) 683–1545

ARCHIVIST:
Sr. Emma Cecilia Busam, OSU

AREA INCLUDED IN DIOCESE:
Allen, Ballard, Breckinridge, Butler, Caldwell, Calloway, Carlisle, Christian, Crittenden, Daviess, Edmonson, Fulton, Graves, Grayson, Hancock, Henderson, Hickman, Hopkins, Livingston, Logan, Lyon, McCracken, McLean, Marshall, Muhlenberg, Ohio, Simpson, Todd, Trigg, Union, Warren, and Webster counties.

Requests may be directed to the archives (located at the Pastoral Center) or to the parish of origin, if known. There are two diocesan cemeteries in Owensboro: Mater Dolorosa and Resurrection. The Cemeteries Office is located at 5404 Leitchfield Rd., Owensboro, KY, 42303. Many of the older parishes in the diocese have their own cemeteries; record keeping for them is done at the parish level. The archivist for the diocese, Sr. Emma Cecilia Busam, OSU, is also the archivist for the Mount St. Joseph Archives (Maple Mount, KY, 42356). The Mount St. Joseph Archives contain the Ursuline Motherhouse Annals, materials from the Sister of Loretto convent and school which preceded the Ursuline house, records from the Mount St. Joseph Girl's Academy, Kentucky oral histories and artifacts, a growing genealogy collection, and general Kentucky histories.

FEES:
Donations are accepted.

DIOCESAN HISTORY:
The Diocese of Western Kentucky (1994).

This Far by Faith: The Story of Catholicity in Western Kentucky 1937-1987 (1987) by Judy Hayden.

CATHOLIC NEWSPAPER:
The Western Kentucky Catholic
600 Locust St.
Owensboro, KY 42301

Est. 1984. May be searched at the newspaper offices by appointment. The newspaper is also on file at the diocesan archives.

LOUISIANA

ARCHDIOCESE OF NEW ORLEANS

Historical Archives
1100 Chartres St.
New Orleans, LA 70116–2596
Telephone: (504) 529–2651

AREA INCLUDED IN DIOCESE:

The following civil parishes in the state of Louisiana: Jefferson, Orleans, Plaquemines, St. Bernard, St. Charles, St. John the Baptist, St. Tammany, and Washington.

Sacramental records for the Archdiocese of New Orleans have been published by the Archdiocesan Historical Archives and are available for purchase at $30.00 per volume.

Sacramental Records Vol. 1 (1718–1750)
Sacramental Records Vol. 2 (1751–1771)
Sacramental Records Vol. 3 (1772–1783)
Sacramental Records Vol. 4 (1784–1790)
Sacramental Records Vol. 5 (1791–1795)
Sacramental Records Vol. 6 (1796–1700)
Sacramental Records Vol. 7 (1800–1803)
Sacramental Records Vol. 8 (1804–1806)
Sacramental Records Vol. 9 (1807–1809)

These volumes contain detailed indexes to baptisms, marriages, and funerals recorded during the years covered. All sacramental acts that indicate a surname are included. Information about parents, baptismal sponsors, and marriage witnesses is included. Cross-references are included for maiden/married surnames, pseudonyms, combination names, and significant surname variations. Many records reflect the Spanish policy of including detailed information about the grandparents of baptized infants.

Make checks payable to the Archdiocesan Historical Archives. All volumes postpaid. Orleans Parish residents add nine percent sales tax; other Louisiana residents add four percent sales tax. Cash, check, or money order must accompany order. No purchase orders. Send orders to the Archdiocesan Historical Archives at the above address.

FEES:

$5.00 per certified copy of sacramental records.

DIOCESAN HISTORY:

Cross, Crozier, Crucible (1993) by Glenn Conrad.

The Catholic Church in Louisiana (1939) by Roger Baudier.

DIOCESE OF ALEXANDRIA

Archives
4400 Coliseum Blvd.
P.O. Box 7417
Alexandria, LA 71306
Telephone: (318) 445–2401

AREA INCLUDED IN DIOCESE:

The civil parishes of Avoyelles, Catahoula, Concordia, Franklin, Grant, LaSalle, Madison, Natchitoches, Rapides, Tensas, Vernon, and Winn.

The Diocese of Alexandria was first established as the Diocese of Natchitoches in 1853. In 1910 it was moved to Alexandria and became the Diocese of Alexandria. Records of all churches in the diocese are on microfilm, which is housed at the diocesan archives. Early records of Natchitoches have been microfilmed and are housed at Northwestern State University in Natchitoches.

FEES:

$10.00 for the first hour of research; $3.00 for every hour thereafter. Certificates may be obtained, on completion of the initial research, for $3.00 each.

DIOCESE OF BATON ROUGE

Department of the Archives
P.O. Box 2028
Baton Rouge, LA 70821
Telephone: (504) 387–0561 (for information only)

AREA INCLUDED IN DIOCESE:

The civil parishes of Ascension, Assumption, East Baton Rouge, East Feliciana, Iberville, Livingston, Pointe Coupee, St. Helena, St. James, Tangipahoa, West Baton Rouge, and West Feliciana.

The Department of the Archives is the repository of the sacramental records of the Catholic churches within the Diocese of Baton Rouge. Baptismal, marriage, and burial information from the church records is available to researchers at a nominal fee. Archival holdings generally do not include records after 1900. These records are still housed at the individual churches. The following records, grouped by civil parish, are in the archives for safekeeping:

Acadian Registers
- Three registers of the parish of St. Charles-aux-Mines at Grand-Pre in Acadia (1707–1748). These books, carried by Acadians who were expelled from their homeland, survived through years of exile, and were eventually brought to St. Gabriel by Acadian settlers.

Ascension Parish
- Ascension Church, Donaldsville; baptisms (1772–1924), marriages (1722–1906), burials (1772–1906)
- St. Francis of Assisi, Smoke Bend; baptisms (1884–1912), marriages (1884–1917), burials (1892–1952)
- St. Theresa, Gonzales; baptisms (1863–1905), marriages (1864–1912), burials (1863–1908)

Assumption Parish
- Assumption Church, Plattenville; baptisms (1793–1947), marriages (1793–1947), burials (1793–1943)
- St. Elizabeth, Paincourtville; baptisms (1844–1931), marriages (1839–1917), burials, (1844–1914)
- St. Philomena, Labadieville; baptisms (1848–1902), marriages (1849–1909), burials (1851–1911)
- St. Anne, Napoleonville, Baptisms (1874–1928), marriages (1874–1910), burials (1874–1929; 1884–1891 missing)
- Immaculate Conception, Canal; baptisms (1857–1948), marriages (1858–1931; 1887–1919 missing), burials (1857–1948)
- St. Joseph, Pierre Part; baptisms (1858–1921), marriages (1858–1924), burials (1864–1927; 1865–1885 missing)
- St. Gertrude, Bertrandville; baptisms (1896–1899), marriages (1896–1899), burials (1896–1899)

East Baton Rouge Parish
St. Joseph, Baton Rouge; baptisms (1793–1911), marriages (1788–1911), burials (1793–1912; 1815–1818 and 1870–1894 missing). The St. Joseph holdings include registers of marriages at Natchez and in the Feliciana parishes. They also include a number of entries for non-Catholic marriages in which Catholic priests acted as civil administrators under a Spanish decree of 1792.

Iberville Parish
- St. Gabriel, St. Gabriel; baptisms (1773–1919), marriages (1779–1919), burials (1779–1947; 1869–1893 missing)
- St. John the Evangelist, Plaquemine; baptisms (1850–1904), marriages (1850–1909), burials (1858–1867; 1845–1907 missing)
- Our Lady of Prompt Succor, White Castle; baptisms (1899–1907), marriages (1899–1906)
- St. Joseph, Grosse Tete; baptisms (1883–1904), marriages (1888–1902)
- St. Paul, Bayou Goula; baptisms (1877–1929), marriages (1877–1923), burials (1877–1929)

Livingston Parish
- St. Joseph, French Settlement; baptisms (1839–1904), marriages (1874–1906), burials (1873–1917)

Pointe Coupee Parish
- St. Mary, New Roads (includes the records of St. Francis of Pointe Coupee); baptisms (1727–1901; 1814–1837 missing), marriages (1727–1904), burials (1727–1913)
- Immaculate Conception, Lakeland; baptisms (1857–1915), marriages (1861–1915), burials (1861–1937)

• St. Ann, Morganza; baptisms (1875–1899), marriages (1875–1918), burials (1883–1949)

St. James Parish
• St. James, St. James; baptisms (1770–1937), marriages (1770–1937), burials (1770–1937; 1857–1873 missing)
• St. Michael, Convent; baptisms (1809–1913), marriages (1809–1894; some to 1911), burials (1808–1948)
• St. Mary, Union; baptisms (1886–1918), marriages (1887–1918)
• St. Joseph, Paulina; baptisms (1882–1925)
• Our Lady of Peace, Vacherie; baptisms (1856–1923), marriages (1856–1901), burials (1866–1949)
• St. Philip, Vacherie; baptisms (1873–1895), marriages (1873–1920), burials (1873–1954)

Tangipahoa Parish
• St. Dominic, Husser; baptisms (1865–1941), marriages (1870–1940)
• St. Joseph, Ponchatoula; baptisms (1876–1908), marriages (1878–1908), burials (1895–1908)
• Mater Delorosa, Independence; baptisms (1895–1907), marriages (1899–1907)
• St. Helena, Amite; baptisms (1891–1913), marriages (1868–1908), burials (1868–1908)

West Baton Rouge Parish
• St. John the Baptist, Brusly; baptisms (1841–1890; 1871–1874 missing), marriages (1876–1915; 1880–1891 missing), burials (1846–1938; 1866–1892 missing)
• Holy Family Church, Port Allen; baptisms (1876–1929), marriages (1876–1957), burials (1920–1975)

West Feliciana Parish
• Our Lady of Mt. Carmel, St. Francisville; baptisms (1851–1915), marriages (1849–1915), burials (1814–1912)

All of the eighteenth century entries and most of the nineteenth century entries that could be indexed by surname have been abstracted and indexed. Fourteen volumes of the abstracts covering the years through 1879 have been published and may be purchased as described below. Additional volumes are in preparation.

Vol. 1 Acadian Records of St. Charles-aux-Mines, Grand Pre in Acadia (1707–1748) and St. Francis of Point Coupee (1728–1769)
Vol. 2 Colonial Period (1770–1803)
Vol. 3 (1804–1819)
Vol. 4 (1820–1829)
Vol. 5 (1830–1839)
Vol. 6 (1840–1847)
Vol. 7 (1848–1852)
Vol. 8 (1853–1857)
Vol. 9 (1858–1862)
Vol. 10 (1863–1867)
Vol. 11 (1868–1870)
Vol. 12 (1871–1873)
Vol. 13 (1874–1876)
Vol. 14 (1877–1879)

Cash, check, or money order must accompany order. $26.00 per volume plus shipping and handling: $3.00 for the first book, $1.00 for each additional book. Louisiana residents must include sales tax.

When making requests to the archives, it is most helpful if you can include the civil parish (or the church parish) where the family was located and approximate dates of the records requested.

FEES:
Certificates for which no research is required can be obtained for $3.50 for the first certificate and $3.00 for each additional certificate in the same order. Photocopies of the original records from microfilm are available for $7.50 per copy. One photocopy and a typed certificate is $10.00. If the original is too poor to reproduce, your money will be returned. Research on an individual basis in $6.00 for the first hour, each additional hour costs $5.00.

Research, such as ancestor charts or family group sheets, may be done by mail or in person. If done in person, an appointment is required since all work is done in association with a member of the archives staff. Please do not make requests by telephone. Note that it is necessary to pay in advance. A check or money order should be made payable to the Diocese of Baton Rouge.

DIOCESE OF HOUMA-THIBODAUX

Historical Research Center
205 Audubon Ave.
Thibodaux, LA 70301
Telephone: (504) 446–2383

AREA INCLUDED IN DIOCESE:
The civil parishes of La Fourche, Terrebone, and parts of Jefferson and St. Mary.

In 1979 the Diocese of Houma-Thibodaux established an archival program, and in 1983 the Historical Research Center was dedicated. The center is located on the Nicholls State University campus in Thibodaux, Louisiana. Parish records prior to and including 1910 can now be found only in the Historical Research Center. The earliest such register dates back to 1817, when St. Joseph Parish in Thibodaux was officially established. These parish registers contain the following information: birth, baptism, confirmation, marriage, death and burial documentation. Certified copies of records are available at the center. Because of the high degree of interest in genealogy, the Historical Research Center also has a small collection of published family genealogies and welcomes the donations of such publications.

The archives is in possession of the Parish Registers from the following churches:
  St. Joseph, Thibodaux, est. 1817
  St. Francis, Houma, est. 1847
  St. Lawrence, Chacahoula, est.1848
  St. Mary's, Raceland, est. 1850
  Holy Savior, Lockport, est. 1850

  Sacred Heart, Morgan City, est. 1859
  Sacred Heart, Montegut, est. 1864
  Our Lady of the Rosary, Larose, est. 1873
  St. Eloi, Theriot, est. 1875
  Our Lady of Prompt Succor, Chackbay, est. 1892
  St. Ann's, Bourg, est. 1908
  St. Charles Borromeo, Thibodaux, est. 1912
  St. Bridget's, Schriever, est. 1912
  Our Lady of Prompt Succor, Golden Meadow,
    est. 1916
  St. John's, Thibodaux, est. 1919

Research in the archives is done only by research personnel. Should a search involve more than twenty minutes, a fee will be charged. Before contacting the archives, the diocese advises checking *South Louisiana Records*, by the Rev. Donald J. Hebert (Hebert Publications, P.O. Box 147, Rayne, LA 70578), for the record. (The abstract is also included in many library genealogical sections.) The *South Louisiana Records* is an abstract in alphabetical form of the entries found in the registers at the archives, and it can be found in most large genealogical libraries. All sacramental records after 1910 should be obtained from the parish church.

FEES:
For certified records, $5.00 each for the first two copies and $3.00 for additional copies in the same order. Normally, records requested are sent by return mail. A bill accompanies the records. If the charges are not remitted within a month, no further records will be sent by mail. A copy of the information on a file card may be obtained for a fee of $2.50 (not a certified document).

The Historical Research Center is open Monday, Tuesday, and Thursday from 8 A.M to 4 P.M.

DIOCESE OF LAFAYETTE

Archives
1408 Carmel Ave.
Lafayette, LA 70501–5298
Telephone: (318) 261–5639

ARCHIVIST:
Regina Arnaud

AREA INCLUDED IN DIOCESE:
The civil parishes of Acadia, Evangeline, Iberia, Lafayette, St. Landry, St. Martin, St. Mary (west of the Atchafalaya River), and Vermilion.

The Diocese of Lafayette was established in 1918. All sacramental records through approximately 1910 have been included in the Rev. Donald J. Hebert's *Southwest Louisiana Records*, an abstract in alphabetical form of the entries found in southwestern Louisiana parish registers. The books are available from Hebert Publications, P.O. Box 147, Rayne, LA, 70578. (The abstract is also included in many library genealogical sections.) Certificates are issued by the parish of origin. The archives staff does not conduct genealogical research but will direct individuals to the appropriate parish.

FEES:
Determined by the parish.

DIOCESE OF LAKE CHARLES

414 Iris St.
Lake Charles, LA 70601
Telephone: (318) 439–7400

AREA INCLUDED IN DIOCESE:
The civil parishes of Allen, Beauregard, Calcasieu, Cameron, and Jefferson Davis.

Sacramental records are located in the parish churches. There are no baptismal records in the Archives. *Southwest Louisiana Records* by the Rev. Donald J. Hebert, is the most accurate source of Catholic records for the area. These volumes contain abstracts, in alphabetical form, of the entries found in the parish registers of southern Louisiana (Hebert Publications, P.O. Box 147, Rayne, LA, 70578). Certificates are issued at the parish level.

FEES:
Determined by the parish.

DIOCESE OF SHREVEPORT

Catholic Center
2500 Line Ave.
Shreveport, LA 71104
Telephone: (318) 222–2006

ARCHIVIST:
Christine Rivers

AREA INCLUDED IN DIOCESE:
The civil parishes of Bienville, Bossier, Caddo, Claiborne, DeSoto, East Carroll, Jackson, Lincoln, Morehouse, Ouachita, Red River, Richland, Sabine, Union, Webster, and West Carroll.

Sacramental records and early history of individual churches reside with the churches. There was only one parish in what is now the Diocese of Shreveport before 1900. The parent diocese (Diocese of Alexandria) retains all early historical records. Requests for records should be made at the parish level. If the parish is not known, the chancery may be able to help determine one, provided sufficient information is given.

FEES:
Determined by the parish.

DIOCESE OF PORTLAND IN MAINE

510 Ocean Avenue
Woodfords P.O. Box 6750
Portland, ME 04101
Telephone: (207) 773–6471

ARCHIVIST:
Sr. Therese Pelletier

AREA INCLUDED IN DIOCESE:
The state of Maine

Sacramental records are kept by the parishes; there are no baptismal records in the archives. The diocese can often help to locate a particular parish if precise information is provided.

FEES:
Determined by the parish.

CATHOLIC NEWSPAPER:
The Church World
Industry Rd.
P.O. Box 698
Brunswick, ME 04011

Est. 1930. Copies from 1930 are on microfilm at the diocesan archives.

ADDITIONAL MAINE RESOURCES:

PATTEN FREE LIBRARY

Maine History & Genealogy Room
33 Summer St.
Bath, ME 04530

COLLECTION INCLUDES:
• Calvary Cemetery name and dates lists notebook, along with lists of the other two large cemeteries in Bath where Catholics are buried
• Local newspaper obituaries and weddings index, 1781–1914, 1986–present; indexing of the gap from 1914–1985 in progress

ARCHDIOCESE OF BALTIMORE

Chancery Office
320 Cathedral Street
Baltimore, MD 21201
Telephone: (410) 547–5446

AREA INCLUDED IN DIOCESE:

Allegany, Anne Arundel, Baltimore, Carroll, Frederick, Garrett, Hartford, Howard counties and the city of Baltimore.

The Diocese of Baltimore was the first Catholic diocese in the United States. When established in 1789, it included the entire country. Records were transferred to new dioceses as they were created. Original sacramental records are kept by the parishes. Microfilm of sacramental records for approximately seventy-five parishes (mostly Baltimore city churches established before 1900) are available for public use at the Maryland State Archives in Annapolis. The central archives has no records of use genealogical researchers. Certificates are issued by the parish of origin.

FEES:

Determined by the parish. Most researchers are referred to the microfilm at the Maryland State Archives.

DIOCESAN HISTORY:

The Premier See: A History of the Archdiocese of Baltimore 1789–1989 (1989) by Thomas W. Spalding.

CATHOLIC NEWSPAPER:

The Catholic Review
P.O. Box 777
Cathedral St.
Baltimore, MD 21203

Est. 1915. Only carried a few obituaries, so generally not helpful to genealogists. The earlier paper for the diocese was *The Catholic Mirror*, 1850–1908. Newspapers are on microfilm at the main branch of the Enoch Pratt Library in Baltimore.

ARCHDIOCESE FOR MILITARY SERVICE, U.S.A.

962 Wayne Ave.
Silver Spring, MD 20910
Telephone: (301) 853–0400

AREA INCLUDED IN DIOCESE:

All U.S. military bases worldwide, including the U.S. Military Academy at West Point, New York, the U.S. Air Force Academy at Colorado Springs, Colorado, the U.S. Naval Academy at Annapolis, Maryland, and the U.S. Coast Guard Academy at New London, Connecticut.

The Archdiocese for Military Services (formerly known as the Military Ordinariate or Military Vicariate) was founded in 1917 to serve active and reserve military personnel of the United States and their dependents. The archdiocese maintains the records of sacraments performed on U.S. military bases worldwide.

ADDITIONAL MARYLAND RESOURCES:

MARYLAND HISTORICAL SOCIETY

201 West Monument St.
Baltimore, MD 21201

COLLECTION INCLUDES:
- Records of New Cathedral Cemetery, Baltimore (microfilm)
- Microfilm copies of some sacramental records deposited by the Archdiocese of Baltimore with the Maryland State Archives in Annapolis
- *Catholic Families of Southern Maryland, Records of Catholic Residents of St. Mary's County in the Eighteenth Century*, by Timothy J. O'Rourke
- *Maryland Catholics on the Frontier, The Missouri and Texas Settlements*, by Timothy J. O'Rourke
- The papers of Charles Carroll of Carrollton, the only Catholic signer of the Declaration of Independence.

ENOCH PRATT FREE LIBRARY

400 Cathedral St.
Baltimore, MD 21201

COLLECTION INCLUDES:
- *Catholic Mirror*, 1852–1904 (not all years)
- *Baltimore Catholic Review*, 1913 to date

PEABODY LIBRARY

Johns Hopkins University
17 East Mt. Vernon Place
Baltimore, MD 21202

COLLECTION INCLUDES:
- Extensive collection of Baltimore parish registers in published form
- Cemetery records
- Numerous published sources on colonial Maryland, many of which pertain to Catholic families (St. Mary's County)

MASSACHUSETTS

ARCHDIOCESE OF BOSTON

Archives
2121 Commonwealth Ave.
Brighton, MA 02135
Telephone: (617) 254-0100

ARCHIVIST:
Ronald D. Patkus

AREA INCLUDED IN DIOCESE:
Essex, Middlesex, Norfolk, Plymouth, and Suffolk counties, with the exception of the towns of Marion, Mattapoisett, and Wareham.

Researchers may visit the archives or write to us for information.

FEES:
None

DIOCESAN HISTORY:
History of the Archdiocese of Boston 1604-1943 (1944) by Robert H. Lord, et al.

CATHOLIC NEWSPAPER:
The Pilot
49 Franklin St.
Boston, MA 02110

Est. 1829. *The Pilot* is the oldest Catholic newspaper in the United States. Microfilm copies are in the Boston Public Library and at the archives of the archdiocese. Not indexed.

DIOCESE OF FALL RIVER

Chancery Office
P.O. Box 2577
Fall River, MA 02722–2577
Telephone: (508) 675–3850

AREA INCLUDED IN DIOCESE:
Bristol, Barnstable, Dukes, and Nantucket counties, and the towns of Marion, Mattapoisett, and Wareham in Plymouth County.

Sacramental records for the Diocese of Fall River are retained at the parish level. Requests should be directed to the parish of origin. The Chancery can often be of help in determining a parish if precise information is supplied.

FEES:
Determined by the parish.

CATHOLIC NEWSPAPER:
The Anchor
P.O. Box 7
Fall River, MA 02722

Est. 1957. Papers may be researched at *The Anchor* offices. Available from 1957.

DIOCESE OF SPRINGFIELD

Chancery Office
76 Elliot
Springfield, MA 01105
Telephone: (413) 732–3175

AREA INCLUDED IN DIOCESE:
Berkshire, Franklin, Hamden, and Hampshire counties.

All sacramental records for the Diocese of Springfield are kept at the parish level. There is no central archives.

FEES:
Determined by the parish.

CATHOLIC NEWSPAPER:
The Catholic Observer
P.O. Box 1730
Springfield, MA 01101

Est. 1954. Preceded by the *Catholic Mirror Magazine* (1920–1954), *The Observer* (1954–1974) is on file at the Connecticut Valley Historical Museum, 220 State St., Springfield, MA, 01103. The newspapers may also be viewed at the newspaper office by appointment.

DIOCESE OF WORCESTER

49 Elm Street
Worcester, MA 01609
Telephone: (508) 791–7171

AREA INCLUDED IN DIOCESE:
Worcester county.

Sacramental records are maintained at the parish level, where any certificates are issued. Requests should be directed to the parish of origin, if known. The chancery can often be of help in determining a parish if sufficient information is provided.

FEES:
None

CATHOLIC NEWSPAPER:
The Catholic Free Press
49 Elm St.
Worcester, MA 01609

Est. 1951. On file at Assumption College in Worcester and at the Worcester Public Library. They may also be inspected at the newspaper offices. Not indexed. Prior to 1951, Worcester was a part of the Springfield Diocese and would have been covered by the *Catholic Mirror Magazine*.

MICHIGAN

ARCHDIOCESE OF DETROIT

Archives
1234 Washington Blvd.
Detroit, MI 48226
Telephone: (313) 237–5800

ARCHIVIST:

Roman P. Godzak

AREA INCLUDED IN DIOCESE:

Lapeer, Macomb, Monroe, Oakland, St. Clair, and Wayne counties. Early sacramental records have been microfilmed and are available at the Detroit Public Library. It is against diocesan policy to issue certificates for genealogical purposes.

FEES:

Not applicable.

DIOCESAN HISTORY:

Seasons of Grace: A History of the Catholic Archdiocese of Detroit (1990) by Leslie Woodcock Tentler.

The Catholic Church in Detroit 1701–1888 (1951) by Rev. George Pare.

CATHOLIC NEWSPAPER:

The Michigan Catholic
305 Michigan Ave.
Detroit, MI 48226

Est. 1872. Available to researchers at the Detroit Public Library. Not indexed.

DIOCESE OF GAYLORD

1665 M-32 West
Gaylord, MI 49735
Telephone: (517) 732–5147

ARCHIVIST:

Rev. Gerald Micketti

AREA INCLUDED IN DIOCESE:

Alcona, Alpena, Antrim, Benzie, Charlevoix, Cheboygan, Crawford, Grand Traverse, Emmet, Iosco, Kalkaska, Leelanau, Manistee, Montmorency, Missaukee, Ogemaw, Oscoda, Ostego, Presque Isle, Roscommon, and Wexford counties. Sacramental records are retained at the parish level, with copies at the archives.

FEES:

None

CATHOLIC NEWSPAPER:

The Catholic Weekly
P.O. Box 1405
Saginaw, MI 48605–1405

Est. 1938 as *The Saginaw Catholic*. Bound volumes for all years are available at the newspaper offices. The office also has the Gaylord edition back to 1972 and the Lansing edition back to 1955 (at a different site).

DIOCESE OF GRAND RAPIDS

Diocesan Archives
660 Burton St. S.E.
Grand Rapids, MI 49507–3290
Telephone: (616) 243–0491

AREA INCLUDED IN DIOCESE:

Ionia, Kent, Lake, Mason, Mecosta, Montcalm, Muskegan, Newaygo, Oceana, Osceola, and Ottawa countries.

Sacramental records for the diocese are retained at the parish level, with copies at the archives. Requests may be directed to the chancery if the parish is not known.

FEES:

$5.00 per certificate located.

DIOCESE OF KALAMAZOO

Chancery
215 North Westnedge Ave.
P.O. Box 949
Kalamazoo, MI 49005
Telephone: (616) 349–8714

AREA INCLUDED IN DIOCESE:

Allegan, Barry, Berrien, Branch, Calhoun, Cass, Kalamazoo, St. Joseph, and Van Buren counties.

Sacramental records for the diocese are maintained by the parishes. Requests for certificates or genealogical information should be directed to the parish of origin. If an individual can supply complete information, the chancery can often help to determine a parish where records might be found.

FEES:

None

DIOCESE OF LANSING

300 W. Ottawa
Lansing, MI 48933
Telephone: (517) 342–2440

ARCHIVIST:

Rev. George C. Michalek

AREA INCLUDED IN DIOCESE:

Clinton, Eaton, Genesee, Hillsdale, Ingham, Jackson, Lenawee, Livingston, Shiawassee, and Washtenaw counties.

Sacramental records for the Diocese of Lansing are kept at the parishes. The archives maintains records for the churches that have been closed. If the parish is known, requests should be made at that level. The archives office is only open on Tuesdays.

FEES:

None

DIOCESAN HISTORY:

Golden Jubilee: Diocese of Lansing Parish Historical Sketches (1987) by Rev. George C. Michalek.

CATHOLIC NEWSPAPER:

The Catholic Times
P.O. Box B
Flint, MI 48504

Est. 1991. Formerly *The Catholic Weekly* (1954-1990). Both papers are available in bound volumes at the newspaper offices.

DIOCESE OF MARQUETTE

444 South 4th St.
P.O. Box 550
Marquette, MI 49855
Telephone: (906) 225–1141

AREA INCLUDED IN DIOCESE:

The Diocese of Marquette comprises the upper peninsula of the state of Michigan.

Sacramental records for the diocese are maintained at the parish level, where any certificates are issued. If the parish is not known requests may be directed to the diocese. Complete information will help in determining a parish where any records might be located.

FEES:

Donations of $5.00 to $10.00 are appreciated for research time.

DIOCESAN HISTORY:

History of the Diocese of Sault Ste. Marie and Marquette (1906) by Rev. Antione Ivan Rezek.

DIOCESE OF SAGINAW

5800 Weiss St.
Saginaw, MI 48603–2799
Telephone: (517) 799–7910

AREA INCLUDED IN DIOCESE:

Arenac, Bay, Clare, Gladwin, Gratiot, Huron, Isabella, Midland, Saginaw, Sanilac, and Tuscola counties.

Requests for sacramental records are usually handled by the parish of origin.

FEES:

Determined by the parish.

CATHOLIC NEWSPAPER:

The Catholic Weekly
P.O. Box 1405
Saginaw, MI

Est. 1938 as *The Saginaw Catholic*. Bound volumes for all years are available at the newspaper offices. The office also has the Gaylord edition back to 1972 and the Lansing edition back to 1955 (at a different site).

ADDITIONAL MICHIGAN RESOURCES:

POLISH GENEALOGICAL SOCIETY OF MICHIGAN

c/o Burton Historical Collection
Detroit Public Library
5201 Woodward Ave.
Detroit, MI 48202

The Polish Genealogical Society of Michigan is currently re-creating an index of burials (via transcription of headstones) at the oldest Polish Catholic cemetery in Detroit. Sacred Heart Cemetery contains burials of more than 10,000 Catholics (primarily Polish). The first burials occurred in 1894, and they continue today. The transcription process is approximately ninety-five percent complete; the oldest part of the cemetery, still to be done, has many completely buried headstones.

BURTON HISTORICAL COLLECTION

Detroit Public Library
5201 Woodward Ave.
Detroit, MI 48202

COLLECTION INCLUDES:

• Microfilm of Catholic sacramental records for many of the parishes in the Archdiocese of Detroit.
• A massive biographical collection that includes obituaries and death notices of many area Catholics.

ARCHDIOCESE OF ST. PAUL AND MINNEAPOLIS

226 Summit Ave.
St. Paul, MN 55102–2197
Telephone: (651) 291–4429

ARCHIVIST:
Mr. Stephen Granger

ARCHIVES ASSISTANT:
Patrick Anzelc

AREA INCLUDED IN DIOCESE:
Anoka, Carver, Chisago, Dakota, Goodhue, Hennepin, Le Seur, Ramsey, Rice, Scott, Washington, and Wright counties.

All parish records within the Archdiocese of St. Paul and Minneapolis have been microfilmed and are on file at the archives (original registers remain at the parishes). The archives also has parish histories of almost every parish in the archdiocese, as well as some of the parish histories from North and South Dakota. The microfilm collection also includes historical newspapers from the area. The archival assistant usually handles requests for genealogical information. Researchers are welcome.

FEES:
$3.00 per day to use the microfilm personally; $8.50 per hour if the research is done by the archival assistant.

CATHOLIC NEWSPAPER:
The Catholic Bulletin
244 Dayton Ave.
St. Paul, MN 55102

Est. 1911. On microfilm at the Minnesota Historical Society in St. Paul and at the archdiocesan archives. Research may also be done on site at the newspaper offices. An earlier paper, *The Northwest Chronicle*, is available in bound volumes at the Seminary of the University of St. Thomas, in St. Paul.

DIOCESE OF CROOKSTON

1200 Memorial Dr.
P.O. Box 610
Crookston, MN 56716
Telephone: (218) 281–4533

AREA INCLUDED IN DIOCESE:
Becker, Beltrami, Clay, Clearwater, Hubbard, Kittson, Lake of the Woods, Mahnomen, Marshall, Norman, Pennington, Polk, Red Lake, and Roseau counties.

Sacramental data for the parishes within the diocese is on microfilm. All cemeteries are part of individual parish corporations; their records reside with the parishes.

FEES:
Depends upon request.

CATHOLIC NEWSPAPER:
Our Northland Diocese
P.O. Box 610
Crookston, MN 56716

Est. 1946. Bound copies are kept at the newspaper offices and are available for research. Not indexed.

DIOCESE OF DULUTH

2830 E. 4th St.
Duluth, MN 55812
Telephone: (218) 724–9111

AREA INCLUDED IN DIOCESE:
Aitkin, Carlton, Cass, Cook, Crow Wing, Itasca, Koochiching, Lake, Pine, and St. Louis counties.

Records in the archives date from 1936 on; records from before that time are located at the parish level.

If the parish is known, requests may be sent directly to the parish.

FEES:
Donations are appreciated for research time.

DIOCESE OF NEW ULM

Catholic Pastoral Center
1400 Sixth North St.
New Ulm, MN 56073
Telephone: (507) 359–2966

AREA INCLUDED IN DIOCESE:
Big Stone, Brown, Chippewa, Kandiyohi, Lac Qui Parle, Lincoln, Lyon, McLeod, Meeker, Nicollet, Redwood, Renville, Sibley, Swift, and Yellow Medicine counties.

All parish records for the diocese were microfilmed and are at the Diocesan Archives. At present, there is no microfilm reader available for researchers. Microfilms are available for researchers at the Family History Library of the LDS Church and its family history centers. Microfilmed records up to the year 1925, for the churches in Brown County are held by the Brown County Historical Society. At present, individuals who want copies of baptismal certificates must contact the parish of origin.

FEES:
Some parishes charge a small fee—generally $5.00 to $10.00.

CATHOLIC NEWSPAPER:
The Prairie Catholic
1400 Sixth North St.
New Ulm, MN 56073

Est. 1971. Copies may be viewed at the newspaper offices.

DIOCESE OF ST. CLOUD

214 Third Ave. South
P.O. Box 1248
St. Cloud, MN 56302
Telephone: (320) 251–2340

ARCHIVIST:
Msgr. Vincent Yzermans

AREA INCLUDED IN DIOCESE:
Benton, Douglas, Grant, Isanti, Kanabec, Mille Lacs, Morrison, Otter Trail, Pope, Sherburne, Stearns, Stevens, Todd, Traverse, Wadena, and Wilkin counties.

Each parish in the diocese maintains its own records. Some are also maintained at the diocese. Contact the parish of origin directly if known.

FEES:
Donation to cover expenses. If a large amount of time is required, there are charges to pay for the time.

DIOCESAN HISTORY:
The Spirit in Central Minnesota by Msgr. Vincent A. Yzerman

CATHOLIC NEWSPAPER:
The St. Cloud Visitor
P.O. Box 1068
St. Cloud, MN 56302

Est. 1938 as the *St. Cloud Register*. From 1891 to 1894 the first bishop published a newsletter for priests: *The Diocese of St. Cloud: Official Record and Messenger*. A family magazine was published from 1916 to 1919: *My Message*. The Minnesota Historical Society of St. Paul is currently microfilming the papers. *The Visitor* may also be researched at the newspaper offices by appointment.

DIOCESE OF WINONA

Pastoral Center
55 West Sanborn St.
P.O. Box 588
Winona, MN 55987
Telephone: (507) 454–4643

AREA INCLUDED IN DIOCESE:

Blue Earth, Cottonwood, Dodge, Faribault,
Fillmore, Freeborn, Houston, Jackson, Martin,
Mower, Murray, Nobles, Olmstead, Pipestone, Rock,
Steele, Wabasha, Waseca, Watonwan, and Winona
counties.

Early records for the diocese are housed at the
Pastoral Center.

FEES:

None. Donations appreciated.

CATHOLIC NEWSPAPER:

The Courier
P.O. Box 949
Winona, MN 55987

Est. 1912. The paper was not published from 1923
to 1943. Researchers may view the papers at the
newspaper offices by appointment. Not indexed.

DIOCESE OF BILOXI

120 Reynoir St.
P.O. Box 1189
Biloxi, MS 39533
Telephone: (601) 374–0222

AREA INCLUDED IN DIOCESE:
Covington, Forrest, George, Greene, Hancock, Harrison, Jackson, Jefferson Davis, Jones, Lamar, Lawrence, Marion, Pearl River, Perry, Stone, Walthall, and Wayne counties.

Sacramental records for the Diocese of Biloxi are retained at the parish level. Contact the parish of origin. If the parish is not known, the diocese may be able to help determine a parish if sufficient information is provided.

FEES:
Determined by the parish.

DIOCESE OF JACKSON

237 East Amite St.
P.O. Box 2248
Jackson, MS 39225–2248
Telephone: (601) 969–1880

ARCHIVIST:
Mrs. Frances Boeckman

AREA INCLUDED IN

DIOCESE:
Adams, Alcorn, Amite, Attala, Benton, Bolivar, Calhoun, Carroll, Chickasaw, Choctaw, Claiborne, Clarke, Clay, Coahoma, Copiah, De Soto, Franklin, Grenada, Hinds, Holmes, Humphreys, Issaquena, Itawamba, Jasper, Jefferson, Kemper, Lafayette, Lauderdale, Leake, Lee, Leflore, Lincoln, Lowndes, Madison, Marshall, Monroe, Montgomery, Neshoba, Newton, Noxubee, Oktibbeha, Panola, Pike, Pontotoc, Prentiss, Quitman, Rankin, Scott, Sharkey, Simpson, Smith, Sunflower, Tallahatchie, Tate, Tippah, Tishomingo, Tunica, Union, Warren, Washington, Webster, Wilkinson, Winston, Yalobusha, and Yazoo counties.

The archives of the Diocese of Jackson is not staffed for genealogical searches. The sacramental records are considered private and confidential. Occasionally, the part-time archivist has time to search for a specific item but not for a list of items.

FEES:
$15.00 per hour.

DIOCESAN HISTORY:
Christ the Living Water: The Catholic Church in Mississippi (1989) by Cleta Ellington.

The Catholic Church in Mississippi 1837–1865 (1964) by Rev. James J. Pillar, OMI.

Catholicity in Mississippi (1939) by Rev. Richard Oliver Gerow.

MISSOURI

ARCHDIOCESE OF ST. LOUIS

4445 Lindell Blvd.
St. Louis, MO 63108
Telephone: (314) 533–1887

AREA INCLUDED IN DIOCESE:

Franklin, Jefferson, Lincoln, Perry, St. Charles, St. Francois, St. Louis, St. Louis City, Ste. Genevieve, Warren, and Washington counties.

Sacramental records for the Archdiocese of St. Louis are maintained at the parish level, where any certificates are issued. Contact the parish of origin, if known. The archives does not perform genealogical research. Sacramental records for the archdiocese have been microfilmed by the Genealogical Society of Utah and are available to researchers at the Family History Library in Salt Lake City and through its family history centers.

FEES:

Determined by the parish; usually $5.00 per certificate.

CATHOLIC NEWSPAPER:

The Saint Louis Review
462 North Taylor Ave.
St. Louis, MO 63108

Est. 1941 as *The St. Louis Register*, renamed *The Saint Louis Review* in 1957. There were a number of earlier Catholic papers for the state, beginning in 1832. Most of the papers are included in the Missouri Newspaper Project of the Missouri State Historical Society in Columbia. Copies of the *Register* and *Review* are available at the St. Louis Public Library, the St. Louis County Public Library, and St. Louis University. Not indexed.

DIOCESE OF JEFFERSON CITY

605 Clark Ave.
P.O. Box 417
Jefferson City, MO 65101
Telephone: (573) 635–9127

AREA INCLUDED IN DIOCESE:

Adair, Audrain, Benton, Boone, Calloway, Camden, Chariton, Clark, Cole, Cooper, Crawford, Gasconade, Hickory, Howard, Knox, Lewis, Linn, Macon, Maries, Marion, Miller, Moniteau, Monroe, Montgomery, Morgan, Osage, Pettis, Phelps, Pike, Pulaski, Putnam, Ralls, Randolph, Saline, Schuyler, Scotland, Shelby, and Sullivan counties.

Sacramental records for the diocese are maintained at the parish level, where any certificates are issued. It is best to contact the parish directly.

FEES:

Determined by the parish.

DIOCESE OF KANSAS CITY– ST. JOSEPH

P.O. Box 419037
Kansas City, MO 64141–6037
Telephone: (816) 756–1850

AREA INCLUDED IN DIOCESE:

Andrew, Atchison, Bates, Buchanan, Caldwell, Carroll, Cass, Clay, Clinton, Daviess, De Kalb, Gentry, Grundy, Harrison, Henry, Holt, Jackson, Johnson, Lafayette, Livingston, Mercer, Nodaway, Platte, Ray, Saint Clair, Vernon, and Worth counties.

Sacramental records for the diocese are located in the parish of origin, with copies at the archives. Records have not been released to libraries or societies, but individuals may research at the archives.

FEES:
The archives charges a copying fee.

DIOCESAN HISTORY:
This Far by Faith: A Popular History of the Catholic People of West and Northwest Missouri (1992, 2 vols.) by Dorothy Marra, et al., can be ordered through the diocesan offices for $50.00 per set. This work covers the period from 1820 through 1990. It includes many photographs, biographical sketches of clergy, histories of the various institutions within the diocese, and locations of various records. It is an excellent source for any kind of research covering the Catholic settlements of western and northern Missouri.

DIOCESE OF SPRINGFIELD– CAPE GIRARDEAU
The Catholic Center
601 South Jefferson St.
Springfield, MO 65806
Telephone: (417) 866–0841

AREA INCLUDED IN DIOCESE:
Barry, Barton, Bollinger, Butler, Cape Girardeau, Carter, Cedar, Christian, Dade, Dallas, Dent, Douglas, Dunklin, Greene, Howell, Iron, Jasper, Laclede, Lawrence, Madison, McDonald, Mississippi, New Madrid, Newton, Oregon, Ozark, Pemiscot, Polk, Reynolds, Ripley, Scott, Shannon, Stoddard, Stone, Taney, Texas, Wayne, Webster, and Wright counties.

The chancery holds copies of sacramental records from 1956 on; records prior to that time are maintained at the parish level. If the parish is known, contact it directly. The diocese can usually be of help in determining a parish if precise information is given.

FEES:
Determined by the parish. Small donations are appreciated.

CATHOLIC NEWSPAPER:
The Mirror
M.P.O. Box 847
Springfield, MO 65801

Est. 1965. On file at the Missouri State Historical Society in Columbia. Papers may also be researched at the newspaper offices.

ADDITIONAL MISSOURI RESOURCES:

ST. LOUIS GENEALOGICAL SOCIETY
9011 Manchester Road, Suite 3
St. Louis, MO 63144–2643

COLLECTION INCLUDES:
- *The St. Louis Genealogical Society's Catholic Marriages, St. Louis, 1774–1840* and *Catholic Baptisms, St. Louis, 1765–1840*, which were compiled from the three Catholic churches in St. Louis during the French and Spanish governments
- The society's volume *Catholic Cemetery Inscriptions of Jefferson County, Missouri,* relates to Jefferson County, adjacent to St. Louis County on the south (mostly Slavic and Bohemian burials, 1871–1983)

Each of these small volumes is available from the society for $6.15 postpaid.

MISSOURI STATE HISTORICAL SOCIETY
Missouri Newspaper Project
1020 Lowry St.
Columbia, MO 65201

COLLECTION INCLUDES:
- Copies of papers for all dioceses within the state of Missouri; including German and Czech papers out of the Archdiocese of St. Louis. Several of the papers date from the mid–1800s.

DIOCESE OF GREAT FALLS

Catholic Pastoral Center
Box 1399
121 23rd St. South
Great Falls, MT 59403
Telephone: (406) 727–6683

ARCHIVIST:
Rev. Dale McFarlane

AREA INCLUDED IN DIOCESE:
Big Horn, Blaine, Carbon, Carter, Cascade, Chouteau, Custer, Daniels, Dawson, Fallon, Fergus, Hill, Garfield, Golden Valley, Judith Basin, Liberty, Mc Cone, Musselshell, Park, Petroleum, Phillips, Powder River, Prairie, Richland, Roosevelt, Rosebud, Sheridan, Stillwater, Sweet Grass, Treasure, Valley, Wilbaux, Yellowstone, and parts of Teton and Toole counties.

The Diocese of Great Falls tries to answer all queries; however, material in the archives is limited. Cramped quarters make it necessary for visitors to make an appointment.

FEES:
A minimal fee is assessed.

CATHOLIC NEWSPAPER:
The Harvest
Catholic Pastoral Center
Box 1399
Great Falls, MT 59403

Est. 1985. Preceded by *The Great Falls Catholic Review* (1917–1931) and *The Montana Catholic Register* (1931–1985). Papers may be researched at the newspaper offices. Not indexed.

DIOCESE OF HELENA

515 North Ewing
P.O. Box 1729
Helena, MT 59624
Telephone: (406) 442–5820

AREA INCLUDED IN DIOCESE:
Beaverhead, Broadwater, Deer Lodge, Flathead, Gallatin, Glacier, Granite, Jefferson, Lake, Lewis and Clark, Lincoln, Madison, Meagher, Mineral, Missoula, Pondera, Powell, Ravalli, Sanders, Silver Bow, Wheatland, and parts of Teton and Toole counties.

Historical research is done on a time-available basis only. Presently, most of the early sacramental records are kept at the parish level with a few at the diocese. The diocese does maintain microfilm copies of baptisms and marriages. The Cemeteries Office, located at the chancery offices, has information for Catholic cemeteries in Butte, Helena, and Missoula. Several of the parishes within the diocese also have cemeteries; records for these are maintained at the parish level.

FEES:
Donations are accepted. If an individual can provide sufficient information so that the record is immediately accessible, there is no fee. A general search requires $10.00 per hour and a $50.00 deposit.

DIOCESAN HISTORY:
Go With Haste Into The Mountains (1984) by Cornelia M. Flaherty

CATHOLIC NEWSPAPER:
The Montana Catholic
P.O. Box 1729
Helena, MT 59624

Est. 1985. Preceded by the original *Montana Catholic* (1897-190?), *The Catholic Bulletin* (1921-1932), *The Register* (1932-1972), and *The WestMont Word* (1972-1985). Some of the papers are housed at the newspaper offices and may be viewed there by appointment.

ADDITIONAL MONTANA RESOURCES:

YELLOWSTONE GENEALOGY FORUM

c/o Parmly Billings Library
510 N. Broadway
Billings, MT 59101

COLLECTION INCLUDES:
• Listings of gravestone inscriptions from all known Catholic cemeteries in Yellowstone County. These include Assumption Catholic Cemetery, Calvary Catholic Cemetery, Holy Cross Catholic Cemetery, and St. Anthony/Laurel Catholic Cemetery. Assumption Catholic Church Cemetery is actually located just inside Stillwater County but is included because so many residents of Yellowstone County were buried in this cemetery. Broadview, where the cemetery is located, is near the corner of four counties so residents from these counties may be buried there. Calvary Catholic Cemetery and Holy Cross Catholic Cemetery are both located in Billings. Some graves have been moved from Calvary to Holy Cross, which was established in 1954. St. Anthony Catholic Cemetery and Laurel Cemetery lie next to each other in Laurel, with no real distinction made between the two with the exception of marker placement.

• The Yellowstone Genealogy Forum also has listings for four funeral homes in the county with an alphabetized index.

BUTTE-SILVER BOW PUBLIC LIBRARY

226 West Broadway
Butte, MT 59701

COLLECTION INCLUDES:
• St. Patrick's Cemetery sextons' records (earliest Catholic Cemetery in Butte)
• Butte city directories, 1885-present
• Irish and "Butte Irish" materials
• Montana census, 1860–1920

BUTTE-SILVER BOW PUBLIC ARCHIVES

P.O. Box 81
17 West Quartz St.
Butte, MT 59703
Telephone: (406) 723–8262

COLLECTION INCLUDES:
• Butte birth and death records
• Cemetery records, including Catholic cemeteries
• Church histories
• Records from Ancient Order of Hibernians (Irish Catholic)
• City Directories
• Mortuary records

NEBRASKA

ARCHDIOCESE OF OMAHA

Chancery Office
100 North 62nd St.
Omaha, NE 68132
Telephone: (402) 558–3100

AREA INCLUDED IN DIOCESE:
Antelope, Boone, Boyd, Burt, Cedar, Colfax, Cuming, Dakota, Dixon, Dodge, Douglas, Holt, Knox, Madison, Merrick, Nance, Pierce, Platte, Sarpy, Stanton, Thurston, Washington, and Wayne counties.

Sacramental records within the archdiocese are maintained at each parish. Requests should be directed to the parish of origin.

FEES:
Determined by the parish.

CATHOLIC NEWSPAPER:
The Catholic Voice
N.W. Radial Hwy.
P.O. Box 4010
Omaha, NE 68104–0010

Est. 1903. Microfilms copies of the papers (all years) are housed at the Omaha Public Library and the Nebraska State Library (Archives) in Lincoln. They are not indexed for marriage or obituaries.

DIOCESE OF GRAND ISLAND

P.O. Box 1531
Grand Island, NE 68802
Telephone: (308) 382–6565

ARCHIVIST:
L.L. Wernhoff

AREA INCLUDED IN DIOCESE:
Arthur, Banner, Blaine, Box Butte, Brown, Buffalo, Cherry, Cheyenne, Custer, Dawes, Deuel, Garden, Garfield, Grant, Greeley, Hooker, Howard, Keya Paha, Kimball, Logan, Loup, McPherson, Morrill, Rock, Scotts Bluff, Sheridan, Sherman, Sioux, Thomas, Valley, and Wheeler counties and those parts of Dawson, Hall, Lincoln, and Keith counties lying north of the South Platte River. The diocoese is 40,000 square miles.

Some of the records are at the archives, but most are kept in the individual parishes. The diocese has eighty-five churches.

FEES:
Determined by the parish.

CATHOLIC NEWSPAPER:
The West Nebraska Register
P.O. Box 608
Grand Island, NE 68802

Est. 1930. Papers may be viewed at the newspaper offices by appointment.

DIOCESE OF LINCOLN

3400 Sheridan Blvd.
P.O. Box 80328
Lincoln, NE 68501–0328
Telephone: (402) 488–0921

ARCHIVIST:

Sr. Loretta Gosen

AREA INCLUDED IN DIOCESE:

Adams, Butler, Cass, Chase, Clay, Dundy, Fillmore, Franklin, Frontier, Furnas, Gage, Gosper, Hamilton, Harlan, Hayes, Hitchcock, Jefferson, Johnson, Kearney, Lancaster, Nemaha, Nuckolls, Otoe, Pawnee, Perkins, Phelps, Polk, Red Willow, Richardson, Saline, Saunders, Seward, Thayer, Webster, and York counties and those parts of Dawson, Hall, Lincoln, and Keith counties lying south of the Platte River.

Copies of the sacramental records for the Diocese of Lincoln are housed in the diocesan archives.

FEES:

Contact the Archivist

DIOCESAN HISTORY:

Pre-Statehood History of the Catholic Church in Southern Nebraska (1992).

History of the Diocese of Lincoln: 1887-1987 (1992) by Sr. Loretta Gosen.

NEVADA

DIOCESE OF RENO-LAS VEGAS

515 Court St.
P.O. Box 1211
Reno, NV 89504
Telephone: (702) 329–9274

AREA INCLUDED IN DIOCESE:
The entire state of Nevada.
All documents are kept in the Reno chancery office.

FEES:
None

NEVADA HISTORICAL SOCIETY

1650 N. Virginia Street
Reno, NV 89503

COLLECTION INCLUDES:
- Microfilm of the *Nevada Register*, 1953–1956 and from 1960
- Gravestone lists for some of the early Nevada Catholic cemeteries
- Extensive files of one Reno funeral home and a twenty-year collection of obituaries of individuals whose funerals were handled by another funeral home, most of which were Catholic
- WPA volume: *Inventory of the Church Archives of Nevada: Roman Catholic Church*

DIOCESE OF MANCHESTER

153 Ash Street
P.O. Box 310
Manchester, NH 03105
Telephone: (603) 669–3100

DIOCESE OF MANCHESTER-MUSEUM

140 Laurel St.
Manchester, NH 03103
Telephone: (603) 624–1729

ARCHIVIST
Ms. Judith Fosher

AREA INCLUDED IN DIOCESE:
The entire state of New Hampshire. The diocesan museum houses parish histories, many of the early sacramental records for the Diocese of Manchester, and other items of historical interest to researchers. Inquiries may be directed to the museum or to the chancery office. Researchers are welcome.

FEES:
There is no set fee, but donations are appreciated.

ARCHDIOCESE OF NEWARK

171 Clifton Ave.
Newark, NJ 07104–0500
Telephone: (973) 596–4000

AREA INCLUDED IN DIOCESE:

Bergen, Essex, Hudson, and Union counties.

The sacramental records for the Archdiocese of
Newark have been microfilmed by the Genealogical
Society of Utah and are available for researchers at
the Family History Library in Salt Lake City and its
family history centers. Baptismal certificates can be
obtained from the parish origin.

FEES:

Decided at the parish level.

DIOCESE OF CAMDEN

1845 Haddon Ave.
P.O. Box 709
Camden, NJ 08101–0709
Telephone: (609) 756–7900

AREA INCLUDED IN DIOCESE:

Atlantic, Camden, Cape May, Cumberland,
Gloucester, and Salem counties.

Researchers should begin their search at the parish
level. If the parish is in question, the diocese can
often be of help in determining a parish if sufficient
information is provided.

FEES:

None

CATHOLIC NEWSPAPER:

The Catholic Star Herald
1845 Haddon Ave.
Camden, NJ 08101–0709

Est. 1951. Bound copies are housed at the newspaper offices. Research may be done by appointment.

DIOCESE OF METUCHEN

P.O. Box 191
Metuchen, NJ 08840
Telephone: (908) 283–3800

AREA INCLUDED IN DIOCESE:

Hunterdon, Middlesex, Somerset, and Warren
counties.

Records are maintained at the parish level.

FEES:

Determined by the parish.

CATHOLIC NEWSPAPER:

The Monitor
315 Lowell Ave.
P.O. Box 3095
Trenton, NJ 08619

DIOCESAN CEMETERIES:

Resurrection Burial Park
P.O. Box 189
899 Lincoln Ave.
Piscataway, NJ 08855–0189

Holy Cross Burial Park
P.O. Box 1000
840 Cranbury Rd.
Jamesburg, NJ 08831

DIOCESE OF PATERSON

777 Valley Road
Clifton, NJ 07013
Telephone: (973) 777–8818

ARCHIVIST:
Rev. Raymond J. Kupke

AREA INCLUDED IN DIOCESE:
Morris, Passaic, and Sussex counties.
Sacramental records are maintained at the parish level.

FEES:
None.

DIOCESAN HISTORY:
Living Stories: A History of the Catholic Church in the Diocese of Paterson (1987) by Raymond J. Kupke.

CATHOLIC NEWSPAPER:
The Beacon
P.O. Box 1887
Clifton, NJ 07015

Est. 1967. Before that time the area was covered by the *Advocate* out of Newark. Copies of *The Beacon* may be inspected at the newspaper offices by appointment.

DIOCESE OF TRENTON

701 Lawrence Rd.
P.O. Box 5309
Trenton, NJ 08638–0309
Telephone: (609) 394–5666

AREA INCLUDED IN DIOCESE:
Burlington, Mercer, Monmouth, and Ocean counties.

Records within the chancery were destroyed by a fire in 1956. Requests for records should be directed to the parish of origin. The chancery can often help to locate a parish where records might be located if sufficient information is provided.

FEES:
Determined by the parish.

DIOCESAN HISTORY:
Catholic Churches in the Diocese of Trenton, NJ (1906) by Rev. Walter T. Leahy.

Upon This Rock (1993) by Rev. Msgr. Joseph C. Shenrock (editor).

NEW MEXICO

ARCHDIOCESE OF SANTA FE

Catholic Center
4000 St. Joseph Pl. N.W.
Albuquerque, NM 87120
Telephone: (505) 831–8100

AREA INCLUDED IN ARCHDIOCESE:

Colfax, Curry, DeBaca, Guadalupe, Harding, Los Alamos, Mora, Quay, Roosevelt, San Miguel, Santa Fe, Socorro, Taos, Torrance, and Union counties and parts of Bernalillo, Sandoval, Rio Arriba, and Valencia counties.

The Archdiocese of Santa Fe did not supply information requested for this guide. However, sacramental records for the archdiocese have been microfilmed by the Genealogical Society of Utah and are available for researching at the Family History Library in Salt Lake City and related family history centers. Microfilm of the same records is also available to researchers at the University of New Mexico's Center for Southwest Research in Albuquerque, (1678–1869).

DIOCESAN HISTORY:

Lamy Memorial Centenary of the Archdiocese of Santa Fe 1850–1950 (1950) by Bishop Edwin V. Byrne.

CATHOLIC NEWSPAPER:

The People of God
1800 Martha N.E.
Albuquerque, NM 87112

Est. 1982.

DIOCESE OF GALLUP

711 South Puerco Dr.
P.O. Box 1338
Gallup, NM 87305
Telephone: (505) 863–4406

AREA INCLUDED IN DIOCESE:

Catron, Cibola, McKinley, San Juan, and part of Rio Arriba, Sandoval, Bernalillo, and Valencia counties in New Mexico; also Apache and Navajo counties and those parts of the Navajo and Hopi reservations in Coconino County in Arizona.

Most of the sacramental records remain at the individual parishes. St. Michael's Mission has the Navajo family records. If the parish is known, contact it directly. The chancery office can often provide leads on requests of this type. Each request for records is considered individually.

FEES:

Determined by the parish.

CATHOLIC NEWSPAPER:

The Voice of the Southwest
P.O. Box 1421
Gallup, NM 87305

Est. 1969. Very few obituaries, no marriage news. Researchers are welcome.

DIOCESE OF LAS CRUCES

1280 Med Park
Las Cruces, NM 88004
Telephone: (505) 523–7577

AREA INCLUDED IN DIOCESE:

Chaves, Dona Ana, Eddy, Grant, Hidalgo, Lea, Lincoln, Luna, Otero, and Sierra counties.

All sacramental records are kept at the parish level.

FEES:

Determined by the parish.

ADDITIONAL NEW MEXICO RESOURCES:

CENTER FOR SOUTHWEST RESEARCH

University of New Mexico
General Library
Albuquerque, NM 87131–1466

COLLECTION INCLUDES:

• Microfilm copies of sacramental records, Archdiocese of Santa Fe, 1678–1860
• New Mexico Catholic newspapers
• University of Albuquerque yearbooks (incomplete)

NEW YORK

ARCHDIOCESE OF NEW YORK

1011 First Ave.
New York, NY 10022
Telephone: (212) 371–1000

ARCHIVIST:
Sr. Marguerita Smith

AREA INCLUDED IN DIOCESE:
The boroughs of Manhattan, Bronx, and Richmond in New York City and Dutchess, Orange, Putnam, Rockland, Sullivan, Ulster, and Westchester counties.

All sacramental records are stored at the parish level. Direct requests to the parish of origin.

The Calvary and Allied Cemeteries, 1011 First Ave., New York, NY 10022, comprise the diocese's Catholic cemetery association.

FEES:
There are no set fees, but donations are appreciated.

DIOCESAN HISTORY:
A Popular History of the Archdiocese of New York (1983) by Rev. Msgr. Florence D. Cohalen.

CATHOLIC NEWSPAPER:
Catholic New York
1011 First Ave.
New York, NY 10022

Est. 1981. Preceded by *Catholic News*, 1886–1980. Microfilm of both newspapers is housed at St. Joseph's Seminary in Yonkers. May be viewed by appointment.

DIOCESE OF ALBANY

Pastoral Center
40 North Main Ave.
Albany, NY 12203
Telephone: (518) 453–6600

AREA INCLUDED IN DIOCESE:
Albany, Columbia, Delaware, Fulton, Green, Montgomery, Otsego, Rensselar, Saratoga, Schenectady, Schoharie, Warren, Washington countries, and parts of Herkimer and Hamilton counties.

Most of the sacramental records remain at the parish level. Direct requests to the parish of origin, if known. The diocese can often be of help in locating records if precise information is provided.

FEES:
None.

CATHOLIC NEWSPAPER:
The Evangelist
40 North Main Ave.
Albany, NY 12203

Est. 1926. Microfilm of all issues from 1926 to the present is available at the newspaper offices by appointment. Not indexed. There were several earlier newspapers, but few copies remain.

DIOCESE OF BROOKLYN

75 Greene Ave.
P.O. Box C
Brooklyn, NY 11202
Telephone: (718) 399–5900

AREA INCLUDED IN DIOCESE:

Kings and Queens counties.

Sacramental records are maintained at the parish level.

FEES:

Determined by the parish; usually $5.00.

CATHOLIC NEWSPAPER:

The Tablet
653 Hicks St.
Brooklyn, NY 11231

Est. 1908. Copies are available at the Brooklyn Public Library, Main Branch; St. John's University, Jamaica, New York; St. Francis College; Brooklyn, New York, and at the newspaper's main offices.

DIOCESE OF BUFFALO

795 Main St.
Buffalo, NY 14203
Telephone: (716) 847–8700

ARCHIVIST:

Rev. Msgr. Walter Kern

AREA INCLUDED IN DIOCESE:

Allegany, Cattaraugus, Chautauqua, Erie, Genesee, Niagara, Orleans, and Wyoming counties.

The Archives of the Diocese of Buffalo does not do genealogical work, but will provide a list of names and addresses of parishes, with the date of founding and ethnic composition of early members. Each parish retains its sacramental records. The older sacramental records have been microfilmed by the Genealogical Society of Utah and are available at the Family History Library In Salt Lake City and its related family history centers. The same microfilm is also available to researchers at Canisius College in Buffalo. There is no cemeteries office for the diocese; however, the individual cemeteries are quite cooperative, time permitting, in providing information. The archives will provide an address list on request.

FEES:

Each parish has to pay its personnel, so they ask a modest amount ($2.00 to $3.00) unless a large amount of time is required.

CATHOLIC NEWSPAPER:
Western New York Catholic
795 Main St.
Buffalo, NY 14203

Microfilms are available at the Buffalo and Erie County Historical Society, 25 Nottingham Court, Buffalo, NY, 14216. Earlier editions, *The Catholic Union* (1872–1937), *The Catholic Union and Echo* (1937–1964), and *The Magnifcat* (1965–1971), are also on microfilm at the society. The papers carried some obituaries (only a few per issue) in the 1880s into the early 1900s. Most of these were of Irish people, and often the place of birth in Ireland was mentioned. Microfilm is located at the University of Buffalo's Lockwood Library.

DIOCESE OF OGDENSBURG

622 Washington St.
P.O. Box 369
Ogdensburg, NY 13669
Telephone: (315) 393–2920

ARCHIVIST:
Rev. Lawrence E. Cotter

AREA INCLUDED IN DIOCESE:
Clinton, Essex, Fanklin, Jefferson, Lewis, St. Lawrence, and parts of Hamilton and Herkimer counties.

There are few baptismal and marriage records in the archives of the Diocese of Ogdensburg. They are stored at the local parishes, from which certificates can be obtained. The older sacramental records have been microfilmed by the Genealogical Society of Utah and are available at the Family History Library in Salt Lake City and through its family history centers.

FEES:
Determined by at the parish.

DIOCESAN HISTORY:
A History of Catholicism in the North Country (1972) by Sr. Mary Christine Taylor, SSJ.

CATHOLIC NEWSPAPER:
The North County Catholic
P.O. Box 326
Ogdensburg, NY 13669

Est. 1946. Microfilm is available for researchers at Wadhams Hall Seminary College, Riverside Dr., Ogdensburg, NY, 13669. Indexed.

DIOCESE OF ROCHESTER

1150 Buffalo Rd.
Rochester, NY 14624
Telephone: (716) 328–3210

AREA INCLUDED IN DIOCESE:
Cayuga, Chemung, Livingston, Monroe, Ontario, Schuyler, Seneca, Steuben, Tioga, Tompkins, Wayne, and Yates counties.

Original sacramental records are maintained at the parishes where the sacraments were performed. If the parish is known, contact it directly. The older sacramental records have been microfilmed by the Genealogical Society of Utah and are available at the Family History Library in Salt Lake City and through its family history centers.

FEES:
None.

DIOCESAN HISTORY:
Ambassadors for Christ (1994) by Rev. Robert F. McNamara.

The Diocese of Rochester 1868-1968 (1968) by Rev. Robert F. McNamara.

CATHOLIC NEWSPAPER:
The Catholic Courier
1150 Buffalo Rd.
Rochester, NY 14624

Est. 1889. Publication has been continuous but the title has changed over the years. Prior titles have been *The Catholic Journal, Catholic-Courier-Journal,* and *Courier Journal.* Microfilms back to 1889 are housed at Nazareth College, St. Bernard's College, St. John Fisher College, and at the newspaper office. Microfilms may be viewed at the newspaper office by appointment.

DIOCESE OF ROCKVILLE CENTRE
The Chancery
50 North Park Ave.
Rockville Center, NY 11570
Telephone: (516) 678–5800

AREA INCLUDED IN DIOCESE:
Nassau and Suffolk counties (with the exception of Fishers Island). Sacramental records are maintained at the parishes.

FEES:
None

DIOCESAN HISTORY:
Richly Blessed: The Diocese of Rockville Centre 1957-1990 (1991) by Sr. Joan de Lourdes Leonard, CSJ.

CATHOLIC NEWSPAPER:
The Long Island Catholic
P.O. Box 700
115 Greenwich St.
Hempstead, NY 11551

Est. 1962. Too recent to be of genealogical value. Prior to 1962, the area was covered by the *Brooklyn Tablet.*

DIOCESE OF SYRACUSE
240 E. Onondaga St.
P.O. Box 511
Syracuse, NY 13201
Telephone: (315) 470–1493

ARCHIVIST:
Carl Roesch

AREA INCLUDED IN DIOCESE:
Broome, Chenango, Cortland, Madison, Oneida, Onondaga, and Oswego counties.

Sacramental records for the diocese are kept at the parish level. Direct inquiries to the parish of origin, if known.

FEES:
Determined by the parish.

DIOCESAN HISTORY:
Faith and Friendship: Catholicism in Diocese of Syracuse (1909) by William P.H. Hewitt.

CATHOLIC NEWSPAPER:
The Catholic Sun
257 E. Onondaga St.
Syracuse, NY 13202

Est. 1892. Microfilms for all years are housed at the Onondaga County Library, Main Branch, Syracuse, NY, and at the Diocesan Archives. The papers may also be inspected at the newspaper offices by appointment. Not indexed.

ADDITIONAL NEW YORK RESOURCES:

CANISIUS COLLEGE

Archives
2001 Main Street
Buffalo, NY 14208

COLLECTION INCLUDES:
- Microfilms of early Catholic sacramental records for all eight western New York counties: Allegany, Cattaraugus, Chautauqua, Erie, Genesee, Niagara, Orleans, and Wyoming
- Canisius College yearbooks
- Alumni directory for Canisius College

HAVILAND HEIDGERD HISTORICAL COLLECTION

Elting Library
93 Main Street
New Paltz, NY 12561

COLLECTION INCLUDES:
- Only known list of Delaware and Hudson Canal employees, 1850–1900. Many of the employees were Catholics from Ireland (members of St. Peter's Catholic Church, Rosendale)
- Obituaries from New Paltz newspapers, 1860–present
- Church, cemetery and Bible records

ONONDAGA PUBLIC LIBRARY

The Galleries of Syracuse
447 South Salina St.
Syracuse, NY 13202–2494

COLLECTION INCLUDES:
- Microfilm of *The Catholic Sun*, 24 June 1892-present (incomplete)

FLOWER MEMORIAL LIBRARY

Genealogical Committee
Watertown, NY 13601

COLLECTION INCLUDES:
- Gravestone transcriptions from Catholic cemeteries in the Watertown area.

NORTH CAROLINA

DIOCESE OF CHARLOTTE

P.O. Box 36776
Charlotte, NC 28236
Telephone: (704) 377–6871

AREA INCLUDED IN DIOCESE:

Alexander, Alleghany, Anson, Ashe, Avery,
Buncombe, Burke, Cabarrus, Caldwell, Catawba,
Cherokee, Clay, Cleveland, Davidson, Davie,
Forsyth, Gaston, Graham, Guilford, Haywood,
Henderson, Iredell, Jackson, Lincoln, Macon,
Madison, McDowell, Mecklenberg, Mitchell,
Montgomery, Polk, Randolf, Richmond,
Rockingham, Rowan, Rutherford, Stanley, Stokes,
Surry, Swain, Transylvania, Union, Watauga,
Wilkes, Yadkin, and Yancey counties in western
North Carolina.

The Diocese of Charlotte was established in 1972,
from the Diocese of Raleigh, which included the
entire state of North Carolina. The sacramental
records for the diocese have been microfilmed;
copies are housed in the diocesan archives. The
archives also maintains a clipping file with information on the various parishes. Certificates are issued
by the parish of origin.

FEES:

Determined by the parish. Once the microfilm is
indexed, a fee will be established.

DIOCESAN HISTORY:

*A History of the Early Years of the Roman Catholic
Diocese of Charlotte* (1984) by Sr. Miriam Miller,
OSF.

DIOCESE OF RALEIGH

300 Cardinal Gibbons Drive
Raleigh, NC 27606
Telephone: (919) 821–9729

AREA INCLUDED IN DIOCESE:

Alamance, Beaufort, Bertie, Bladen, Brunswick,
Camden, Carteret, Caswell, Chatham, Chowan,
Columbus, Craven, Cumberland, Currituck, Dare,
Duplin, Durham, Edgecombe, Franklin, Gates,
Granville, Greene, Halifax, Harnett, Hertford,
Hoke, Hyde, Johnston, Jones, Lee, Lenoir, Martin,
Moore, Hash, New Hanover, Northampton,
Onslow, Orange, Pamlico, Pasquotank, Pender,
Perquimans, Person, Pitt, Robeson, Sampson,
Scotland, Tyrrell, Vance, Wake, Warren, Washington,
Wayne, and Wilson counties in eastern North
Carolina.

Sacramental records are maintained at the parish
level. Some of the early records are also on file at the
North Carolina Department of Archives in Raleigh.

FEES:

Determined by the parish.

NORTH DAKOTA

DIOCESE OF BISMARK

Center for Pastoral Ministry
520 North Washington St.
P.O. Box 1137
Bismark, ND 58502–1137
Telephone: (701) 222–3035

ARCHIVIST:
Mr. Kenneth Small

AREA INCLUDED IN DIOCESE:
Adams, Billings, Bowman, Burke, Burleigh, Divide, Dunn, Emmons, Golden Valley, Grant, Hettinger, McKenzie, McLean, Mercer, Morton, Mountrail, Oliver, Renville, Sioux, Slope, Stark, Ward, and Williams counties.

Most of the sacramental records remain at the parishes. If the parish is known, individuals should begin their research at that level. Baptismal records are also on microfilm at the chancery. When the parish is unknown, the diocese can often be of help if accurate information is supplied.

FEES:
None.

CATHOLIC NEWSPAPER:
Dakota Catholic Action
P.O. Box 1137
Bismark, ND 58502

Est. 1941. Papers may be researched at the newspaper offices. Partially indexed.

DIOCESE OF FARGO

1310 Broadway
Box 1750
Fargo, ND 58107
Telephone: (701) 235–6429

AREA INCLUDED IN DIOCESE:
Barnes, Benson, Bottineau, Cass, Cavalier, Dickey, Eddy, Foster, Grand Forks, Griggs, Kidder, LaMoure, Logan, McHenry, McIntosh, Nelson, Pembina, Pierce, Ramsey, Ransom, Richland, Rolette, Sargent, Sheridan, Steele, Stutsman, Towner, Traill, Walsh, and Wells counties.

Sacramental records for the diocese remain at the parishes. Parishes should be contacted directly. The diocese will supply information as to which churches are in particular towns, so that individuals determine a parish where records might be kept.

FEES:
Determined by the parish. Donations accepted for the research time.

ARCHDIOCESE OF CINCINNATI

Historical Archives of the Chancery
6616 Beechmont Ave.
Cincinnati, OH 45230
Telephone: (513) 231–0810

ARCHIVIST:
Mr. Don H. Buske

AREA INCLUDED IN DIOCESE:
Adams, Auglaize, Brown, Butler, Champaign, Clark, Clermont, Clinton, Darke, Greene, Hamilton, Highland, Logan, Mercer, Miami, Montgomery, Preble, Shelby, and Warren counties.

The Historical Archives of the Chancery maintains a master set of Catholic sacramental records, on microfiche, for the nineteen-county area of south-western Ohio over which the Archdiocese presides. Records are not open to the general public, and they may only be handled by authorized personnel. Genealogical researchers have the right to ask for information that is public in nature and pertains to the researcher or his or her ancestors. Individuals seeking genealogical information must submit requests by mail (no exceptions). Requests must contain the following four items:

1. The full name of the individual whose record is desired.
2. The type of record you wish researched (baptism, confirmation, first communion, marriage, and/or death).
3. The approximate date (within three to five years) that the record was created.
4. The exact parish in which the above record was recorded. If the exact parish is unknown, the address or neighborhood of the individual concerned may help to determine the parish. If you are researching a nineteenth century marriage the bride's parish or her parents' address at the time of the wedding are required.

Due to the volume of requests and limited staff time, the archives' staff is unable to do extensive research for genealogists. No more than one hour of staff time can be committed to each request. Note that nineteenth century sacramental records often do not include information considered standard today. For example, marriage records do not always give the dates and places of the spouses' births or the names of their parents.

FEES:
There is a $20.00 fee to help cover the expense of the office and staff for one hour of research. Do not send cash. Make a check or money order payable to the Historical Archives of the Chancery, and allow six to eight weeks for a reply.

DIOCESAN HISTORY:
History of the Archdiocese of Cincinnati 1821–1921 (1921) by Rev. John H. Lamott, STD.

CATHOLIC NEWSPAPER:
Catholic Telegraph
100 East Eighth Street
Cincinnati, OH 45202

Est. 1831. Complete microfilms are available at the University of Dayton, Xavier University, the Cincinnati and Hamilton Public Library, Athenaeum of Ohio, and at the *Telegraph* offices. Not indexed.

DIOCESE OF CLEVELAND

Archives
Room 300, Chancery
1027 Superior Ave.
Cleveland, OH 44114
Telephone: (216) 696–6525

ARCHIVIST:
Rev. Ralph E. Wiatrowski, M. Div., S.T.D.

DIRECTOR OF ARCHIVES:
Chris L. Krosel

AREA INCLUDED IN DIOCESE:
Ashland, Cuyahoga, Geauga, Lake, Lorain, Medina, Summit, and Wayne counties.

Most sacramental records are still retained in the parishes where they were created. Those of closed parishes are maintained by the archives. Sacramental records are closed to researchers, but the staff can extract data for interested persons. The Cemeteries Office, also located at the chancery, maintains the records for the three oldest cemeteries in the city of Cleveland. Parish cemeteries maintain their own records. The *Catholic Universe Bulletin* publishes a yearly directory which gives founding dates, addresses of parishes, and information regarding closed parishes and institutions.

FEES:
Determined by the parish. If the work is done by the central office, the first hour of work is free; each additional hour is $6.50. There is a charge of $2.00 per document.

CATHOLIC NEWSPAPER:
Catholic Universe Bulletin
1027 Superior Ave. N.E.
Cleveland, OH 44114

Est. 1874. Copies are available at the Cleveland Public Library and the Ohio Historical Society in Columbus. Not indexed.

DIOCESE OF COLUMBUS

198 East Broad St.
Columbus, OH 43215
Telephone: (614) 224–2251

AREA INCLUDED IN DIOCESE:
Coshocton, Delaware, Fairfield, Fayette, Franklin, Hardin, Hocking, Holmes, Jackson, Knox, Licking, Madison, Marion, Morrow, Muskingum, Perry, Pickaway, Pike, Ross, Scioto, and Tuscarawas counties.

Requests for genealogical information are usually handled by the Catholic Record Society for the Diocese of Columbus. Only transcriptions of records are available. The oldest records are being published in the monthly *Catholic Record Society Bulletin*. Back issues of the *Bulletin* are available in bound volumes. Society dues are $10.00 per year. Membership includes monthly *Bulletin*, quarterly meetings, and a summer bus trip. The society may be reached at 197 East Gay St., Columbus, OH, 43215.

FEES:
The society has no fixed fees but accepts donations.

CATHOLIC NEWSPAPER:
The Catholic Times
P.O. Box 636
Columbus, OH 43216

Est. 1951. Preceded by *The Catholic Columbian* (1875-1939) and *The Columbus Register* (1940-1951). The papers are on microfilm (1875-present) at the Ohio Dominican College, 1216 Sunbury Rd., Columbus, OH 43219, and at the Ohio Historical Society in Columbus. Not indexed.

DIOCESE OF STEUBENVILLE

422 Washington St.
P.O. Box 969
Steubenville, OH 43952
Telephone: (614) 282–3631

AREA INCLUDED IN DIOCESE:

Athens, Belmont, Carroll, Gallia, Guernsey, Harrison, Jefferson, Lawrence, Meigs, Morgan, Monroe, Noble, and Washington counties.

Sacramental records are maintained at the parish level. Records for closed parishes are housed at the Chancery. Requests should be directed to the parish where the sacrament was performed. When the parish is unknown, providing complete information to the chancery will help in determining a parish where records might be found.

FEES:

None.

CATHOLIC NEWSPAPER:

Steubenville Register
P.O. Box 160
Steubenville, OH 43952

Est. 1942. Papers may be researched at the newspaper offices by appointment.

DIOCESE OF TOLEDO

P.O. Box 985
Toledo, OH 43696
Telephone: (419) 244–6711

ARCHIVIST:

Sr. Nora Klewicki, OSL

AREA INCLUDED IN DIOCESE:

Allen, Crawford, Defiance, Erie, Fulton, Hancock, Henry, Huron, Lucas, Ottawa, Paulding, Putnam, Richland, Sandusky, Seneca, Van West, Williams, Wood, and Wyandot counties.

The Diocesan Archives have a small staff; genealogical searches are not a priority.

FEE:

$3.00 per certificate if precise information is given.
$10.00 per hour if little information is given.

DIOCESAN HISTORY:

The History of the Diocese of Toledo: General History (1983) by Msgr. Lawrence Mossing.

The History of the Diocese of Toledo: Northern Ohio—West Section (1984) by Msgr. Lawrence Mossing.

The History of the Diocese of Toledo: Northern Ohio—West and Central (1986) by Msgr. Lawrence Mossing.

The History of the Diocese of Toledo: Giant in the Diocese of Toledo (1987) by Msgr. Lawrence Mossing.

The History of the Diocese of Toledo: Young Shepherd in the Diocese of Toledo (1988) by Msgr. Lawrence Mossing.

The Diocese of the Diocese of Toledo: The Bishop Alter Years (1989) by Msgr. Lawrence Mossing.

DIOCESE OF YOUNGSTOWN

144 W. Wood St.
Youngstown, OH 44503
Telephone: (330) 744–8451

AREA INCLUDED IN DIOCESE:

Ashtabula, Columbiana, Mahoning, Portage, Stark, and Trumbull counties.

Sacramental records for the diocese are maintained at the parish level, where any certificates are issued. If the parish is unknown, the diocese can often be helpful in determining where records might be located if precise information is provided.

FEES:

Determined by the parish. There is no fee for sacramental purposes.

DIOCESAN HISTORY:

The March of the Eucharist from Dungannon (1951) by Msgr. Rev. James A. McFadden.

CATHOLIC NEWSPAPER:

The Catholic Exponent
P.O. Box 6787
Youngstown, OH 44501-6787

Est. 1944. Preceded by the lay-owned *Catholic Exponent* in the first part of the century. Available for researchers at the Ohio Historical Society in Columbus and at the newspaper offices by appointment.

ADDITIONAL OHIO RESOURCES:

THE OHIO HISTORICAL SOCIETY

I-71 and E. 17th Ave.
Columbus, OH 43211

COLLECTION INCLUDES:

• Newspapers for most of the Ohio dioceses

FAIRFIELD COUNTY CHAPTER

Ohio Genealogical Society
P.O. Box 1470
Lancaster, OH 43130–0570

COLLECTION INCLUDES:

• "Cemeteries of Berre Twp, Fairfield Co., Ohio" is included in the book *St. Mary's Cemetery*. The book is available at the above address for $10.00 and $3.00 postage and handling. (Ohio residents include 5.5 percent sales tax.)

SOUTHERN OHIO GENEALOGICAL SOCIETY

P.O. Box 414
Hillsboro, OH 45133

COLLECTION INCLUDES:

• *Cemetery Inscriptions of Highland Co., Ohio.* Hardbound, surname index, 595 pages, $40.00. Include $2.50 for postage and handling. (Ohio residents add 5.5 percent sales tax.)

OKLAHOMA

ARCHDIOCESE OF OKLAHOMA CITY

P.O. Box 32180
Oklahoma City, OK 73123
Telephone: (405) 721–5651

AREA INCLUDED IN DIOCESE:

Alfalfa, Beaver, Beckham, Blaine, Caddo, Canadian, Carter, Cimarron, Cleveland, Comanche, Cotton, Custer, Dewey, Ellis, Garfield, Garvin, Grady, Grant, Greer, Harmon, Harper, Jackson, Jefferson, Johnston, Kay, Kingfisher, Kiowa, Lincoln, Logan, Love, McClain, Major, Marshall, Murray, Noble, Oklahoma, Pontotoc, Pottawatomie, Roger Mills, Seminole, Stephens, Texas, Tillman, Washita, Woods, and Woodward counties.

With the exception of the newspaper, the Archdiocese of Oklahoma City did not supply information.

CATHOLIC NEWSPAPER:

The Sooner Catholic
P.O. Box 32180
Oklahoma City, OK 73123

Est. 1974. Catholic papers preceding *The Sooner Catholic* can be found at the Oklahoma State Historical Society in Oklahoma City.

DIOCESE OF TULSA

Archives
P.O. Box 2009
Tulsa, OK 74101
Telephone: (918) 587–3115

ARCHIVIST:

Mrs. Rita I. Burns

AREA INCLUDED IN DIOCESE:

Adair, Atoka, Bryan, Cherokee, Choctaw, Coal, Craig, Creek, Delaware, Haskell, Hughes, Latimer, LeFlore, McCurtain, McIntosh, Mayes, Muskogee, Nowata, Okfuskee, Okmulgee, Osage, Ottawa, Pawnee, Payne, Pittsburg, Pushmataha, Rogers, Sequoyah, Tulsa, Wagoner, and Washington counties.

Requests may be directed to the archives if the parish is unknown. Complete information must be supplied for any search to be made.

FEES:

There is no fee for baptismal certificates. Research fees for genealogical purposes will depend on the extent of the request—generally $12.50 per hour.

OREGON

ARCHDIOCESE OF PORTLAND

Archdiocesan Pastoral Center
2838 East Burnside St.
Portland, OR 97214–1895
Telephone: (503) 234–5334

AREA INCLUDED IN DIOCESE:

Benton, Clackamas, Clatsop, Columbia, Coos, Curry, Douglas, Jackson, Josephine, Lane, Lincoln, Linn, Marion, Multnomah, Polk, Tillamook, Washington, and Yamhill counties.

With the exception of the newspaper, the Archdiocese of Portland did not supply information. However, some of the early sacramental records for the area have been published and are available through the St. Paul Mission Historical Society (see Additional Oregon Resources below).

CATHOLIC NEWSPAPER:

Oregon Sentinel
5536 N.E. Hassalo
Portland, OR 97213

Est. 1870. Microfilm copiess of the paper are available at the University of Portland Library and the Oregon Historical Society Library in Portland. Microfilm copies are also housed at the newspaper offices and may be researched there by appointment. Not indexed.

DIOCESE OF BAKER

P.O. Box 5999
Bend, OR 97708
Telephone: (503) 388–4004

AREA INCLUDED IN DIOCESE:

Baker, Crook, Deschutes, Gilliam, Grant, Harney, Hood River, Jefferson, Klamath, Lake, Malheur, Morrow, Sherman, Umatilla, Union, Wallowa, Wasco, and Wheeler counties.

The Diocese of Baker is the smallest diocese in the lower forty-eight states, with less than 30,000 Catholics. Sacramental records are found at the parish level.

FEES:

Determined by the parish.

CATHOLIC NEWSPAPER:

Oregon Sentinel

Est. 1870. See above under Archdiocese of Portland.

ADDITIONAL OREGON RESOURCES:

OREGON STATE LIBRARY

State Library Building
Summer and Court Street, N.E.
Salem, OR 97310

COLLECTION INCLUDES:
- Oregon Cemetery Directory—by county, then name of cemetery. (CS/OR/ 929.3795)
- St. Barbara Cemetery (1863–1957)
- St. Joseph Catholic Church, (Salem, Marin Co.), two death register books (1889–1952) (OSL Microfilm 11–141)
- *Catholic Church Records of the Pacific Northwest*, six volumes: Vancouver, Stellamarie Mission, Grande Ronde, Roseburg/Portland, Oregon City/Salem/Jacksonville; St. Paul; St. Ann/Walla Walla/French Town

OREGON HISTORICAL SOCIETY

1230 S.W. Park Ave.
Portland, OR 97268

COLLECTION INCLUDES:
- Microfilm of *Catholic Sentinel*
- Lenzen, Connie. *St. Mary's Cemetery*
- Munnick's *Catholic Church Records of the Pacific Northwest*
- Microfilm of the Daybook of the Sisters of Notre Dame of St. Paul, from Oregon City, 1848
- Clipping files on area churches, published histories of churches, Jesuit histories, and several books about Catholics in Oregon

ST. PAUL MISSION HISTORICAL SOCIETY

4225 Mission Ave. N.E.
P.O. Box 158
St. Paul, OR 97137–0158

St. Paul Mission is the birthplace of Catholicism in the Pacific Northwest. The Archdiocese of Oregon City, the second archdiocese in the United States, was formed while Archbishop Blanchet was in residence there (1846).

COLLECTION INCLUDES:
Early Catholic newspapers for the area, local Catholic cemetery gravestone inscriptions, and sacramental records for the area up until 1900. The sacramental record books are available for purchase as follows:

- *Catholic Church Records of the Pacific Northwest*, by Harriet Duncan Munnick
- St. Ann, St. Rose, Walla Walla, French Town (one volume)
- Grande Ronde, volumes I and II (in one volume)
- Roseburg, Portland (in one volume)
- Oregon City, Salem, Jacksonville (in one volume)
- St. Louis, Gervais, and Brooks (in one volume)
- St. Paul, volumes I, II, and III (in one volume)
- Vancouver, volumes I, II and Stellamarie Mission

The books are available at the St. Paul Mission Society for $25.00 per copy, plus $2.00 mailing and handling for each book.

GENEALOGICAL SOCIETY OF DOUGLAS COUNTY

P.O. Box 579
Roseburg, OR 97470

COLLECTION INCLUDES:
- Catholic cemetery inscriptions for Douglas County

PENNSYLVANIA

ARCHDIOCESE OF PHILADELPHIA

Archives and Historical Collections
1000 East Wynnewood Road
Overbrook, PA 19096–3001
Telephone: (610) 667–2125

ARCHIVIST:
Joseph J. Casino

AREA INCLUDED IN DIOCESE:
The City of Philadelphia and Bucks, Chester, Delaware, Montgomery, and Philadelphia counties.

The archives contains baptismal and marriage records created before the year 1900 for all parishes presently within the Archdiocese of Philadelphia. In addition to sacramental records, the archives retains a large collection of parish histories, nineteenth century newspapers, city directories, Catholic directories, etc., all of which are open to the public. Sacramental records are private and research on them is conducted by archives staff only.

FEES:
$15.00 for the first hour of research; $10.00 for each additional hour.

CATHOLIC NEWSPAPER:
The Catholic Standard and Times
222 North 17th St.
Philadelphia, PA 19103

Est. 1866. On microfilm at the Ryan Memorial Library, St. Charles Borromeo Seminary (same address as the archives). Earlier papers are *The Catholic Herald* (1833) and *The Catholic Herald and Visitor* (1857). Not indexed.

DIOCESE OF ALLENTOWN

202 North 17th Street
P.O. Box F
Allentown, PA 18105
Telephone: (215) 437–0755

AREA INCLUDED IN DIOCESE:
Berks, Carbon, Lehigh, Northampton, and Schuylkill counties.

Sacramental records for parishes within the Diocese of Allentown are stored at the parish level. Requests should be directed to the parish of origin, if known. The diocese can often be of help in determining a parish if precise information is supplied.

FEES:
None.

DIOCESE OF ALTOONA–JOHNSTOWN

Box 126, Logan Blvd.
Hollidaysburg, PA 16648
Telephone: (814) 695–5579

AREA INCLUDED IN DIOCESE:
Bedford, Blair, Cambria, Centre, Clinton, Fulton, Huntington, and Somerset counties.

Sacramental records for the diocese are maintained at the parish level. Requests may be directed to the parish of origin, if known. The diocese can often be of help in determining a parish if precise information is supplied.

FEES:
Determined by the parish.

CATHOLIC NEWSPAPER:
The Catholic Register
P.O. Box 413
Hollidaysburg, PA 16648

Est. 1934. Microfilms are on file at *The Register* offices for the years 1934–1960. The papers may be researched on a limited basis, by application to the editor. The diocese is currently in the process of updating the archives to make the papers more accessible to researchers.

DIOCESE OF ERIE
St. Marks Catholic Center
P.O. Box 10397
Erie, PA 16514
Telephone: (814) 824–1111

ARCHIVIST:
Rev. Robert G. Barcio, Ph.D.

AREA INCLUDED IN DIOCESE:
Cameron, Clarion, Clearfield, Crawford, Elk, Erie, Forest, Jefferson, McKean, Mercer, Potter, Venango, and Warren counties. Archives for the diocese are located at St. Marks Catholic Center.

FEES:
There is no set fee for certificates, but donations are accepted.

DIOCESAN HISTORY:
A Cathedral in the Wilderness: A history of the Diocese of Erie, 1853-1920 (1991), by Rev. Robert Barcio, is available through the Catholic Center. A second volume for the years 1920-1990 is in progress. Direct inquiries to the Catholic Center.

CATHOLIC NEWSPAPER:
The Lake Shore Visitor
P.O. Box 10668
Erie, PA 16514

Est. 1874. Microfilms are available at the Nash Library, Gannon University, University Square, Erie, PA, 16541. Papers may also be viewed at the newspaper offices. Not indexed.

DIOCESE OF GREENSBURG
723 E. Pittsburgh Street
Greensburg, PA 15601–2697
Telephone: (412) 837–0901

ARCHIVIST:
Ursula J. Donaher

AREA INCLUDED IN DIOCESE:
Armstrong, Fayette, Indiana, and Westmoreland counties.

Requests for information may be sent to the chancery office. If the parish is known, contact it directly.

FEES:
None.

CATHOLIC NEWSPAPER:
The Catholic Accent
P.O. Box 850
Greensburg, PA 15601

Est. 1961. Microfilms of the paper are located at St. Vincent College Library, Latrobe; Seton Hall College Library, Greensburg; and the diocesan archives. Papers may also be viewed at the newspaper offices. News of the Greensburg diocese was covered in *The Pittsburgh Catholic* prior to the founding of *The Accent*.

DIOCESE OF HARRISBURG

4800 Union Deposit Rd.
P.O. Box 2153
Harrisburg, PA 17105
Telephone: (717) 657–4804

ARCHIVIST:
Mrs. Kathleen Signor

AREA INCLUDED IN DIOCESE:
Adams, Columbia, Cumberland, Dauphin, Franklin, Juniata, Lancaster, Lebanon, Mifflin, Montour, Northumberland, Perry, Snyder, Union, and York counties.

Original sacramental records are maintained in the parishes of origin, with microfilm copies at the archives. If the parish is known, contact it directly. When requesting information at the diocesan level, providing complete information will help in determining a parish where any records might be found. A maximum of two hours will be spent per research request.

FEES:
$15.00 for the first hour of research; $5.00 for each half hour thereafter.

CATHOLIC NEWSPAPER:
The Catholic Witness
P.O. Box 2555
Harrisburg, PA 17105

Est. 1966. On file at the diocesan archives from 1966. Papers may also be viewed at the newspaper offices.

DIOCESE OF PITTSBURGH

Diocesan Archives
125 North Craig St.
Pittsburgh, PA 15213
Telephone: (412) 621–6217

AREA INCLUDED IN DIOCESE:
Allegheny, Beaver, Butler, Greene, Lawrence, and Washington counties.

The Diocese of Pittsburgh, established in 1843, was the first diocese established in western Pennsylvania. Sacramental records for the diocese are kept in the individual parishes. The archives receives many requests related to genealogies and can often help locate a specific parish for records. There are over three hundred parishes (churches and missions) in the diocese.

FEES:
Determined by the parish.

DIOCESAN HISTORY:
Shepherd of the Faith, by Msgr. Francis Glenn, is a brief history of the bishops who have served in the diocese. It is available through the diocesan office for $12.00.

CATHOLIC NEWSPAPER:
The Pittsburgh Catholic
100 Wood St., Suite 500
Pittsburgh, PA 15222

Est. 1844. Microfilm copies of the paper are housed at Duquesne University Library, Pittsburgh, PA, 15219 (from 1844). Microfilms are also available at the newspaper offices.

DIOCESE OF SCRANTON

300 Wyoming Avenue
Scranton, PA 18503–1279
Telephone: (717) 346–8910

AREA INCLUDED IN DIOCESE:

Bradford, Lackawanna, Luzerne, Lycoming, Monroe, Pike, Sullivan, Susquehanna, Tioga, Wayne, and Wyoming counties.

Sacramental records are maintained at the parish level, where any certificates are issued. Contact the parish directly, in known. The diocese can often be of help in determining a parish is precise information is supplied.

FEES:
None.

DIOCESAN HISTORY:

Century of Progress, by the diocesan historian, Msgr. John P. Gallagher, covers the first one hundred years of the Diocese of Scranton. Msgr. Gallagher is currently writing a second volume.

FEES:
None.

CATHOLIC NEWSPAPER:

The Catholic Light
300 Wyoming Ave.
Scranton, PA 18503-1279

Est. 1901. Preceded by the *Catholic Record* (1887-1890) and the *Diocesan Record* (1890-1901). Early editions of *The Catholic Light* are available for researchers at the University of Scranton, Harry and Jeanette Weinberg Memorial Library, Scranton, PA, 18510. There are no facilities for inspection at the newspaper offices. Not indexcd.

DIOCESE OF PROVIDENCE

One Cathedral Square
Providence, RI 02903
Telephone: (401) 278–4500

ARCHIVIST:
Rev. Jacques L. Plante

AREA INCLUDED IN DIOCESE:
The state of Rhode Island.

Sacramental records for the diocese are maintained at the parish level, with copies on microfilm at the diocese. (No reader/printer is available for scanning the microfilms.) Requests should be made directly to the parish where the sacrament was administered. The diocese can often be of help in determining a parish if precise information is supplied.

FEES:
None

DIOCESAN HISTORY:
Catholicism in Rhode Island and the Diocese of Providence: 1780–1886 (1982) by Rev. Robert W. Hayman. (A second part is now being prepared.)

Rhode Island Catholicism: A Historical Guide (1984) by Patrick T. Conely.

Catholicism in Rhode Island: The Formative Era (1976) by Patrick T. Conely and Matthew J. Smith.

The Catholic Church in Rhode Island (1936) by Thomas F. Cullen.

The Diocese of Providence: History of the Catholic Church in the New England . . . (1899) by Rev. Austin Downing.

CATHOLIC NEWSPAPER:
The Providence Visitor
184 Broad Street
Providence, RI 02903

Est. 1875. Early copies of the paper are on file at Providence College in Providence and at the Diocesan Archives.

DIOCESE OF CHARLESTON

119 Broad Street
P.O. Box 818
Charleston, SC 29402
Telephone: (843) 723–3488

ARCHIVIST:
Sr. M. Anne Francis Campbell, OLM

AREA INCLUDED IN DIOCESE:
The state of South Carolina.

Records for the parishes other than the cathedral are kept in the individual parishes. Requests for records should be directed to the parish of origin. If the parish is not known, the diocese can sometimes be of help in determining a parish if precise information is supplied.

FEES:
There are no set fees at this time, but donations are suggested for the research time.

DIOCESAN HISTORY:
Diocese of Wheeling 1850-1950 (1950) by Rev. Robert Weiskircher, STL.

SOUTH DAKOTA

DIOCESE OF RAPID CITY

606 Cathedral Dr.
P.O. Box 678
Rapid City, SD 57709
Telephone: (605) 343–3541

ARCHIVIST:
Sr. Celine Erk, OSB

AREA INCLUDED IN DIOCESE:
Bennett, Butte, Corson, Custer, Dewey, Fall River, Gregory, Haakon, Harding, Jackson, Jones, Lawrence, Lyman, Meade, Mellette, Pennington, Perkins, Shannon, Stanley, Todd, Tripp, Washabaugh, and Ziebach counties.

Sacramental records for the Diocese of Rapid City are maintained at the parish level. Requests for records should be directed to the parish, if known. Researchers may also contact the archivist for information. Bear in mind that records for the early years of the diocese are scarce. The people who settled this territory were intent on survival; often, sacraments were not recorded. There is no cemeteries office for the diocese. Cemeteries are located at the individual parishes, where records are maintained.

FEES:
There are no set fees, but donations are suggested for the research time.

DIOCESE OF SIOUX FALLS

Archives/ St. Joseph Cathedral
504 N. Summit
Sioux Falls, SD 57104
Telephone: (605) 334–9861

ARCHIVIST:
Sr. Marcia Bosch, OSB

AREA INCLUDED IN DIOCESE:
Aurora, Beadle, Bon Homme, Brookings, Brown, Brule, Buffalo, Campbell, Charles Mix, Clark, Clay, Codington, Davidson, Day, Deuel, Douglas, Edmunds, Faulk, Grant, Hamlin, Hand, Hanson, Hughes, Hutchinson, Hyde, Jerauld, Kingsbury, Lake, Lincoln, Marshall, McCook, McPherson, Miner, Minnehaha, Moody, Potter, Roberts, Sanborn Spink, Sully, Turner, Union, Walworth, and Yankton counties.

The archives is located in the lower level of St. Joseph Cathedral; requests may be directed there. Several of the parishes have published histories, which may be found at various libraries around the state.

FEES:
There are no set fees, but donations are accepted.

TENNESSEE

DIOCESE OF KNOXVILLE

417 East Erin Dr.
Knoxville, TN 37919
Telephone: (615) 584–3307

AREA INCLUDED IN DIOCESE:
Anderson, Bledsoe, Blount, Bradley, Campbell, Carter, Claiborne, Cocke, Cumberland, Fentress, Grainger, Greene, Hamblen, Hamilton, Hancock, Hawkins, Jefferson, Johnson, Knox, Loudon, McMinn, Marion, Meigs, Monroe, Morgan, Pickett, Polk, Rhea, Roane, Scott, Sequatchie, Sevier, Sullivan, Unicoi, Union, and Washington counties.

Sacramental records for the diocese are maintained at the parish level, where any certificates are issued. The Diocese of Knoxville will, in time, have copies of baptism and marriage records. Contact the parish of origin, if known.

FEES:
Determined by the parish.

DIOCESE OF MEMPHIS

1325 Jefferson Ave.
P.O. Box 41674
Memphis, TN 38174
Telephone: (901) 722–4700

AREA INCLUDED IN DIOCESE:
Benton, Carroll, Chester, Crockett, Decatur, Dyer, Fayette, Gibson, Hardeman, Hardin, Haywood, Henderson, Henry, Lake, Lauderdale, McNairy, Madison, Obion, Shelby, Tipton, and Weakley counties.

Sacramental records for the diocese are maintained at the parish level. Contact the individual parishes. There is no Catholic cemeteries office for the diocese, but the records for Calvary Cemetery in Memphis are in good order from 1880 (some records date from 1867) Contact Calvary Cemetery, 1660 Elvis Presley Blvd., Memphis, TN, 38106.

FEES:
Donations are accepted; some parishes may request a fee.

DIOCESE OF NASHVILLE

2400 Twenty-First Ave. South
Nashville, TN 37212
Telephone: (615) 383–6393

ARCHIVIST:

Ann Krenson, Vice Chancellor for Archives and
Records

AREA INCLUDED IN DIOCESE:

Bedford, Cannon, Cheatham, Clay, Coffee,
Davidson, DeKalb, Dickson, Franklin, Giles,
Grundy, Hickman, Houston, Humphreys, Jackson,
Lawrence, Lewis, Lincoln, Macon, Marshall,
Mawry, Montgomery, Moore, Overton, Perry,
Putnam, Robertson, Rutherford, Smith, Stewart,
Sumner, Trousdale, Van Buren, Warren, Wayne,
White, Williamson, and Wilson counties.

Sacramental records for the diocese are retained at
the parish level, where any certificates are issued.

FEES:

Determined by the parish.

CATHOLIC NEWSPAPER:

The Tennessee Register
2400 Twenty-First Ave. S.
Nashville, TN 37212

Est. 1937. Preceded by *The Southern Catholic* (1876),
Adam (ca. 1885), *The Catholic Journal of the New
South* (1888-1912), *Facts* (1891-1895), *IHS* (ca.
1890), *The Catholic Herald* (1898-1899), *The
Columbian* (1915-1926), and the *Cresset* (1927-1933).
The Register is on file at the newspaper offices. Some
of the papers are also housed at the Tennessee State
Library and Archives, in Nashville.

The Catholic Archives of Texas, located in Austin
(see Diocese of Austin below) is an excellent
resource for researchers with a Catholic heritage in
Texas. In addition to the early sacramental records
of the dioceses of Austin, Brownsville, and Victoria,
the Archives house microfilms of all Catholic news
publications for the state of Texas, parish and diocesan histories, biographical files of the bishops and
clergy in Texas, and a collection of Texana and
Catholic books. Holdings range from Mexican and
Spanish manuscripts of the sixteenth century to
present day Texas.

Very few actual baptismal or other records exist for
Texas immigrants prior to 1840. From 1794 to 1840
only the following Catholic churches existed in the
state of Texas: San Fernando Church in San
Antonio; San Augustan Church in Laredo; Saint
Mary's Church in Victoria; Sacred Heart Church in
Nagocdoches; San Elizario Church in El Paso; and
smaller missions attached to the local churches.
Immigrants to Mexican Texas did not receive
Baptism or marriage outside of these few locations,
but rather swore to the local magistrate that they
would abide by the "tenets of religion of the Roman
Catholic Church."

ARCHDIOCESE OF SAN ANTONIO

Catholic Archives
2718 West Woodlawn Ave.
P.O. Box 28410
San Antonio, TX 78284–4901
Telephone: (512) 734–2620

ARCHIVIST:
Br. Edward Loch, SM

AREA INCLUDED IN ARCHDIOCESE:
Atascosa, Bandera, Bexar, Comal, Dimmit, Edwards, Frio, Gillespie, Gonzales, Guadalupe, Karnes, Kendall, Kerr, Kinney, La Salle (that part of La Salle County north of the Nueces River), Maverick, McMullen (that part of McMullen County north of the Nueces River), Medina, Real, Uvalde, Val Verde, Wilson, and Zavala counties.

The archives of the Archdiocese of San Antonio maintains microfilm copies of sacramental records for the churches within the archdiocese. Researchers are allowed access to the records by appointment. Searches will be performed for those who are unable to come to the archives themselves. Certificates with seals must be obtained from the parish of origin. Confirmation of appointment is suggested.

FEES:
Microfilm records may be searched for a reimbursement fee of $3.00 per hour. Persons who are unable to come to the archives and who wish a search to be made of the records are required to post a deposit of $10.00 per hour ($20.00 minimum). There is no refund on the minimum deposit. Prints from the microfilm are $1.00. For mail orders there is a postage and handling fee; the minimum mail order charge is $2.50.

DIOCESAN HISTORY:
Archdiocese of San Antonio 1874-1974 (1974) by Rev. Msgr. Alexander C. Wangler (editor).

Diamond Jubile, 1874-1949: Archdiocese of San Antonio (1949) by Rev. M.J. Gilbert (editor).

DIOCESE OF AMARILLO

Diocesan Archives/Pastoral Center
P.O. Box 5644
Amarillo, TX 79117
Telephone: (806) 792–2741

ARCHIVIST:
Sr. Christine Jansen

AREA INCLUDED IN DIOCESE:
Armstrong, Briscoe, Carbon, Castro, Childress, Collingsworth, Dallam, Deaf Smith, Donley, Gray, Hall, Hansford, Hartley, Hemphill, Hutchinson, Lipscomb, Moore, Ochiltree, Oldham, Parmer, Potter, Randall, Roberts, Sherman, Swisher, and Wheeler counties.

The Pastoral Center maintains copies of sacramental records for the churches within the diocese. There is also a Diocesan Archives Center which contains exhibit materials and some of the early letters, etc.

FEES:
Donations are requested for sacramental transcripts.

DIOCESAN HISTORY:
Response of the Roman Catholic Church to the Mexican American in West Texas (1976) by Sr. Regina E. Foppe, RSM.

The Creation and Foundation of the Roman Catholic Diocese of Amarillo (1975) by John Michael Harter.

A History of the Catholic Church in the Panhandle-Plains Area of Texas (1954) by Sr. M. Nellie Rooney, OSF.

DIOCESE OF AUSTIN

Catholic Archives of Texas
1600 N. Congress
P.O. Box 13327—Capitol Station
Austin, TX 78711
Telephone: (512) 476–4888

ARCHIVIST:
Ms. Kinga Perzynska

AREA INCLUDED IN DIOCESE:
Bastrop, Bell, Blanco, Brazos, Burleson, Burnet, Caldwell, Coryell, Falls, Hamilton, Hays, Lampasas, Lee, Limestone, Llano, Mason, McLennon, Milan, Mills, Robertson, San Saba, Travis, Washington, and Williamson counties and the part of Fayette County north of the Colorado River.

The Catholic Archives of Texas is the central Catholic archives for the entire state. The archives maintains and opens to the public early sacramental records for the diocese of Austin, Brownsville (baptisms and marriages), and Victoria (baptisms and marriages). The holdings in the collection range from earliest sixteenth century Spanish explorations to present day events. The collection includes Catholic newspapers, photographs, diocese and parish collections, Texana and Catholic books collection, records of The Texas Knights of Columbus Historical Commission, Texas Catholic Historical Society, and records of various religious associations, societies and Catholic clubs throughout Texas. Because the staff is small, patrons are strongly encouraged to come and research genealogical records at the archives. The archives is open to all researchers by appointment only. Before the staff can process a request for genealogical information, the approximate date and location of the person whose record is being sought. Please be as specific as possible. The archives can also provide a list of professional genealogists for the state of Texas.

FEES:
There is no fee for research done by the researcher except for a copying fee of $5.00 for a sacramental record and 20 cents for photocopies of other documents. For extensive genealogical research, a donation of $10.00 per hour is appreciated.

DIOCESE OF BEAUMONT

703 Archie St.
P.O. Box 3948
Beaumont, TX 77704
Telephone: (409) 838–0451

AREA INCLUDED IN DIOCESE:
Chambers, Hardin, Jasper, Jefferson, Liberty, Newton, Orange, Polk, and Tyler counties.

Baptismal certificates must come from the individual parishes.

FEES:
Determined by the parish.

DIOCESAN HISTORY:
The Diocese of Beaumont: The Catholic Story of Southwest Texas (1991) by Rev. James F. Vanderholt, et al.

DIOCESE OF BROWNSVILLE

P.O. Box 2279
Brownsville, TX 78522
Telephone: (512) 542–2501

AREA INCLUDED IN DIOCESE:
Cameron, Hidalgo, Starr, and Willacy counties.

The early sacramental records for the Diocese of Brownsville are on microfilm at the Catholic Archives of Texas. (see the Diocese of Austin). The archives of the Diocese of Brownsville were not available for genealogical studies when this guide was compiled due to a lack of funds for the necessary equipment and personnel.

FEES:
Not applicable. See information on the Catholic Archives of Texas under Diocese of Austin.

DIOCESE OF CORPUS CHRISTI

620 Lipan Street
P.O. Box 2620
Corpus Christi, TX 78403–2620
Telephone: (512) 882–6191

AREA INCLUDED IN DIOCESE:
Aransas, Bee, Brooks, Duval, Jim Hogg, Jim Wells, Kenedy, Kleberg, Live Oak, Nueces, Refugio, San Patricio, Webb, and Zapata counties and parts of La Salle and McMullen counties.

Sacramental records for the diocese are maintained at the parish level, with copies at the chancery. Requests should be directed to the parish, if known.

FEES:
None.

DIOCESE OF DALLAS

P.O. Box 190507
Dallas, TX 75219
Telephone: (214) 528–2240

ARCHIVIST:
Estelle Metzger

AREA INCLUDED IN DIOCESE:
Collin, Dallas, Ellis, Fannin, Grayson, Hunt, Kaufman, Nabarro, and Rockwall counties.

All sacramental books are kept at the parish level, with the exception of three churches that are closed. There is a central file of microfilms for the baptismal files up to 1978. Only information as to the church of baptism is available. The archival department does not assist in genealogical research. The correct name and birth date are necessary for any inquiry. The archives does not issue certificates for genealogical purposes. Baptismal certificates are considered private information.

FEES:
One person will be researched for a fee of $5.00

DIOCESAN HISTORY:
The Diocese of Dallas, 1890-1990: A Century of Faith (1990) by Rev. Msgr. James I. Tucek.

DIOCESE OF EL PASO

499 St. Matthews
El Paso, TX 79907
Telephone: (915) 595–5000

ARCHIVIST:
Pearl Blanche Aguilar

AREA INCLUDED IN DIOCESE:
Brewster, Culberson, El Paso, Hudspeth, Jeff Davis, Loving, Presidio, Reeves, Ward, and Winkler counties.

Baptismal records are kept at the church in which they were performed. A history of the diocese is in the planning stage. Researchers will find items of interest for the El Paso area in the collection of the Catholic Archives of Texas in Austin.

FEES:
There is not set fee, but donations are appreciated.

DIOCESAN HISTORY:
The Anniversary of the Foundation of the Diocese of El Paso, March 3, 1914 (1965) by Bishop Hugh G. Quinn.

DIOCESE OF FORT WORTH

800 West Loop 820 South
Fort Worth, TX 76108
Telephone: (817) 560–3300

AREA INCLUDED IN DIOCESE:
Archer, Baylor, Bosque, Clay, Comanche, Cooke, Denton, Eastland, Erath, Foard, Hardeman, Hill, Hood, Jack, Johnson, Knox, Montague, Palo Pinto, Parker, Shackleford, Somervell, Stephens, Tarrant, Throckmorton, Wichita, Wilbarger, Wise, and Young counties.

Baptismal records are kept in the church where the baptism took place.

FEES:
Determined by the parish.

DIOCESE OF GALVESTON–HOUSTON

1700 San Jacinto St.
Houston, TX 77002

Mailing address:
P.O. Box 907
Houston, TX 77001
Telephone: (713) 659–5461

ARCHIVIST:
Lisa May

AREA INCLUDED IN DIOCESE:
Austin, Brazoria, Fort Bend, Grimes, Harris, Madison, Montgomery, San Jacinto, Walker, and Waller counties.

Copies of sacramental records for the diocese are housed at the archives. The archives does not issue certificates for genealogical purposes, but will issue transcripts of the records. These can be obtained with the official seal of the diocese, for genealogical purposes. There is no index to the records; requests should supply complete information for the record that you wish searched.

FEES:
None

DIOCESAN HISTORY:
125the Anniversary: Diocese of Galveston-Houston, 1847-1972 (1972) by Robert C. Giles.

Diocese of Galveston Centennial, 1847-1947 (1947) by Rev. J.A. Rapp (editor).

History of the Diocese of Galveston, 1847-1874 (1943) by Sr. M. Carmelita Glennon.

DIOCESE OF LUBBOCK

Catholic Center
4620 Fourth
Lubbock, TX 79416

Mailing address:
P.O. Box 98700
Lubbock, TX 79499–8700
Telephone: (806) 792–3943

AREA INCLUDED IN DIOCESE:
Texas: Bailey, Borden, Cochran, Cottle, Crosby, Dawson, Dickens, Fisher, Floyd, Gaines, Garza, Hale, Haskell, Hockley, Jones, Kent, King, Lamb,

Lubbock, Lynn, Motley, Scurry, Stonewall, Terry, and Yoakum counties.

Original sacramental records are kept at the parish level.

FEES:
$2.00

DIOCESE OF SAN ANGELO

804 Ford
San Angelo, TX 76902

Mailing address:
Box 1829
San Angelo, TX 76902
Telephone: (915) 653–2466

AREA INCLUDED IN DIOCESE:
Andrews, Brown Callahan, Coke, Coleman, Concho, Crane, Crockett, Ector, Glasscock, Howard, Irion, Kimble, McCulloch, Martin, Menard, Midland, Mitchell, Nolan, Pecos, Reagan, Runnells, Schleicher, Sterling, Sutton, Taylor, Terrell, Tom Green, and Upton counties.

Sacramental records are maintained at the parish level.

FEES:
None

DIOCESE OF TYLER

1920 Sybil Lane
Tyler, TX 75703
Telephone: (214) 534–1077

AREA INCLUDED IN DIOCESE:
Anderson, Angelina, Bowie, Camp, Cass, Cherokee, Delta, Franklin, Freestone, Gregg, Harrison, Henderson, Hopkins, Houston, Lamar, Leon, Marion, Morris, Nacogdoches, Panola, Rains, Red River, Rusk, Sabine, San Augustine, Shelby, Smith, Titus, Trinity, Upshur, Van Zandt, and Wood counties.

Sacramental records are maintained at the parish level.

FEES:
None

DIOCESE OF VICTORIA

1505 East Mesquite Lane
Victoria, TX 77901

Mailing address:
P.O. Box 4708
Victoria, TX 77903
Telephone: (512) 573–0828

AREA INCLUDED IN DIOCESE:
Calhoun, DeWitt, Goliad, Jackson, Lavaca, Matagorda, Victoria, and Wharton counties and the parts of Colorado and Fayette counties west of the Colorado River.

Sacramental records are maintained at the parish level. Early records (baptisms and marriages) for the diocese are also at the Catholic Archives of Texas (see the Diocese of Austin).

FEES:
$5.00

DIOCESE OF SALT LAKE CITY

Diocesan Pastoral Center
27 C Street
Salt Lake City, UT 84103
Telephone: (801) 328–8641

ARCHIVIST:

Bernice M. Mooney

AREA INCLUDED IN DIOCESE:

The entire state of Utah.

Sacramental records are administered by the chancery and housed in the diocesan archives. The records are not open to researchers but the chancery office will provide information upon request.

FEES:

A nominal fee is charged for requests that require extensive time to search records.

DIOCESAN HISTORY:

Salt of the Earth: The history of the Catholic Diocese of Salt Lake City, 1776-1987 (1992), by Bernice M. Mooney, is available from the Diocesan Resource Center, 226 So. Main St., Salt Lake City, UT 84101, for $13.00 per copy. (hard bound; 546 pages). *Salt of the Earth* includes the names of many Catholic men and women; and, in appendixes, names of all priests and sisters who have served the diocese.

One Hundred and Fifty Years of Catholicity in Utah (1926) by Rev. Louis J. Fries.

The Catholic Church in Utah (1909) by Rev. W.R. (Dean) Harris.

CATHOLIC NEWSPAPER:

The Intermountain Catholic
27 C Street
Salt Lake City, UT 84103

Est. 1889. No index exists, so research is tedious but often rewarding. The issues are on microfilm, and a reader/printer is available in the archives.

VERMONT

DIOCESE OF BURLINGTON

Bishop Brady Center
351 North Ave.
Burlington, VT 05401
Telephone: (802) 658–6110

ARCHIVIST:

William Goss

AREA INCLUDED IN DIOCESE:

The entire state of Vermont.

If the parish is known, it is best to write directly to it. If unknown, inquiries may be sent to the diocese.

FEES:

$3.00 for an official form with the seal of the diocese.

DIOCESAN HISTORY:

One Hundred Years of Achievement by the Catholic Church in the Diocese of Burlington (1953) by Jeremiah K. Durick (editor).

CATHOLIC NEWSPAPER:

Vermont Catholic Tribune
351 North Ave.
Burlington, VT 05401

Est. 1956. Prior to 1956 the diocese was served by the Indiana paper, *Our Sunday Visitor.* Copies of the *Tribune* are on file at the diocesan archives.

VIRGINIA

DIOCESE OF ARLINGTON

200 N. Glebe Rd.
Arlington, VA 22203
Telephone: (703) 841–2500

ARCHIVIST:
Sr. Mary Aileen, IHM

AREA INCLUDED IN DIOCESE:
Arlington, Clarke, Culpepper, Fairfax, Fauquier, Frederick, King George, Lancaster, Loudoun, Madison, Northumberland, Orange, Page, Prince William, Rappahannock, Richmond, Shenandoah, Spotsylvania, Stafford, Warren, and Westmoreland and the cities of Alexandria, Fairfax City, Falls Church, Fredericksburg, Manassas, Manassas Park, and Winchester counties.

Sacramental records for the diocese are maintained at the parish level. Requests for information or certificates should be directed to the parish of origin. Records at the chancery date from 1974. If sufficient information is provided, the diocese can sometimes help to determine a parish where records might be found.

FEES:
None

CATHOLIC NEWSPAPER:
Arlington Catholic Herald
200 N. Glebe Rd., Suite 614
Arlington, VA 22203

Est. 1976. Of little value to genealogists, very few obituaries or marriages. Before 1976 *The Catholic Virginian* covered the state (Diocese of Richmond).

DIOCESE OF RICHMOND

811 Cathedral Place
Richmond, VA 23220–4898
Telephone: (804) 359–5661

AREA INCLUDED IN DIOCESE:
Accomack, Albemarle, Alleghany, Amelia, Amherst, Appomattox, Augusta, Bath, Bedford, Bland, Botetourt, Brunswick, Buchanan, Buckingham, Campbell, Caroline, Carroll, Charles City, Charlotte, Chesterfield, Craig, Cumberland, Dickenson, Dinwiddie, Essex, Floyd, Fluvanna, Franklin, Giles, Gloucester, Goochland, Grayson, Greene, Greensville, Halifax, Hanover, Henrico, Henry, Highland, Isle of Wight, James City, King and Queen, King William, Lee, Louisa, Lunenburg, Mathews, Mecklenberg, Middlesex, Montgomery, Nelson, New Kent, Northampton, Nottoway, Patrick, Pittsylvania, Powhatan, Prince Edward, Prince George, Pulaski, Roanoke, Rockbridge, Rockingham, Russell, Scott, Smyth, Southampton, Surry, Sussex, Tazewell, Washington, Wise, Wythe, and York counties.

Sacramental records for the diocese are stored at the parish level. The Chancery has copies of baptismal records on microfilm but advises contacting the parish where the sacrament was administered.

FEES:
None, but donations are accepted.

CATHOLIC NEWSPAPER:
Catholic Virginian
P.O. Box 26843
Richmond, VA 23261

Est. 1923. Microfilms of the paper are available at the Virginia State Library and at the newspaper offices. Not indexed.

ADDITIONAL VIRGINIA RESOURCES:

CATHOLIC HISTORICAL SOCIETY
OF THE ROANOKE VALLEY

631 N. Jefferson St.
Roanoke, VA 24016

COLLECTION INCLUDES:

- Card file of persons buried at St. Andrew's Cemetery, Roanoke, and of Catholics buried in other cemeteries in the area
- St. Andrew's School graduates, 1897 to 1949
- St. Andrew's School enrollment, 1926 to 1936 and 1944 to 1953
- Annals of the Sisters of Charity's St. Vincent Orphanage, St. Andrew's and Our Lady of Nazareth
- *On the Hill*, a history of St. Andrew's Parish
- *Our Lady of Nazareth*, 1914-1986
- *The Saint Gerard Story*

WASHINGTON

ARCHDIOCESE OF SEATTLE

Archives
910 Marion St.
Seattle, WA 98104
Telephone: (206) 382–4857

ARCHIVIST:
Ms. Chris Taylor

AREA INCLUDED IN ARCHDIOCESE:
Clallam, Clark, Cowlitz, Grays Harbor, Island, Jefferson, King, Kitsap, Lewis, Mason, Pacific, Pierce, San Juan, Skagit, Skamania, Snohomish, Thurston, Wahkiakum, and Whatcom counties in western Washington.

Holdings in the archives date from 1846. They include: the sacramental registers of pioneer priests; dating from 1848, of closed institutions; such as Sacred Heart Orphanage in Briscoe, and the House of the Good Shepherd, as well as duplicate sacramental records for each parish in the archdiocese. Sacramental records are private by nature; general access is restricted to those records created before 1900. Written research requests are preferred.

Some of the very early sacramental records for the Vancouver area have been published in *Catholic Church Records of the Pacific Northwest*, by Harriet D. Munnick. They are available through The St. Paul Mission Historical Society, P.O. Box 158, St. Paul, OR, 97137–0158. The volumes are also included in many genealogical libraries in the area.

FEES:
Usually $3.00 to $5.00

CATHOLIC NEWSPAPER:
The Progress
910 Marion St.
Seattle, WA 98104

Est. 1899 (until 1982 and the *Catholic Northwest Progress*). Copies of the paper are housed at the archives. Contact the archivist for access. The paper is also on file at the Seattle Public Library (1920-present) and at the University of Washington Library (1933 to the present). Not indexed.

DIOCESE OF SPOKANE

1023 West Riverside Ave.
Spokane, WA 99210
Telephone: (509) 358–7330

Mailing Address:
P.O. Box 1453
Spokane, WA 99210–1453

ARCHIVIST:
Fr. Theodore F.X. Bradley

AREA INCLUDED IN DIOCESE:
Adams, Asotin, Columbia, Ferry, Franklin, Garfield, Lincoln, Okanogan, Pend Oreille, Spokane, Stevens, Walla Walla, and Whitman counties.

Sacramental records through 1956 are on microfilm at the Diocesan Archives, with the originals retained at the parish level. Some of the early records have been microfilmed by the Genealogical Society of Utah and are available for viewing at the Family History Library and its family history centers. Early records from the Walla Walla area are included in *Catholic Church Records of the Pacific Northwest*, by Harriet D. Munnick. Available from The St. Paul Mission Historical Society, P.O. Box 158, St. Paul, OR, 97137-0158.

FEES:
There is no set fee, but donations are appreciated.

CATHOLIC NEWSPAPER:
Inland Register
P.O. Box 48
Spokane, WA 99210

Est. 1942. May be viewed at the newspaper offices by appointment.

DIOCESE OF YAKIMA

5301-A Tieton Dr.
Yakima, WA 98908
Telephone: (509) 965–7117

ARCHIVIST:
Mrs. Gayle Miller

AREA INCLUDED IN DIOCESE:
Benton, Chelan, Douglas, Grant, Kittitas, Klickitat, and Yakima counties in eastern Washington.

Sacramental records for the diocese are maintained at the parish level. If the parish is known contact it directly.

FEES:
Decided at the parish.

ARCHDIOCESE OF WASHINGTON, D.C.

Pastoral Center
5001 Eastern Ave.
Washington, D.C. 20017
Telephone: (301) 853–3800

AREA INCLUDED IN DIOCESE:

Washington, D.C. and Calvert, Charles, Montgomery, Prince George, and St. Mary's counties of Maryland.

Sacramental records are maintained at the parishes, where any certificates are issued. Requests should be directed to the parish of origin. If the parish is not known, the archdiocese will supply a list of parishes that were in existence, for the appropriate time period, to which researchers may write.

FEES:

There are no established fees, but donations are accepted.

ADDITIONAL WASHINGTON, D.C. RESOURCES

MARTIN LUTHER KING MEMORIAL LIBRARY

Washington Division
901 G Street N.W., Room 307
Washington, D.C. 20001

COLLECTION INCLUDES:

• Columbian Harmony Society publications which include selected small cemeteries of Washington, D.C.
• *Washington Star Collection*—approximately 13 million clippings; arranged by subject and personal name
• Washington, D.C. city directories—1822–1973
• *Burials in St. Mary's Catholic Cemetery*, Alexandria, Virginia, 1798-1983

West Virginia

Diocese of Wheeling–Charleston

1300 Byron St.
P.O. Box 230
Wheeling, WV 26003
Telephone: (304) 233–0880

Area included in diocese:

The entire state of West Virginia.

Sacramental records for the diocese are maintained at the parish where the sacrament was performed. The chancery maintains the records for closed parishes. Requests for information or certificates should be directed to the parish of origininvolved. The diocese can often be of help in determining a parish if precise information is supplied.

Fees:

Determined by the parish.

Dicoesan history:

Diocese of Wheeling, 1850–1950 (1950) by Rev. Robert Weiskircher.

Catholic newspaper:

The Catholic Spirit
P.O. Box 951
Wheeling, WV 26003

Est. 1934 as the *West Virginia Register* (1934–1969). In 1970 the paper was renamed *The Catholic Spirit*. The Catholic press has been active in West Virginia since the 1870s, with limited distribution of the *Catholic Messenger* in the Parkersburg locality. The first official diocesan paper, *The Church Calendar*, dates from 1895. Copies of the *Calendar* are housed at the West Virginia University Library in Morgantown (1895–1911). Research on the *Catholic Spirit* can be done at the newspaper offices by appointment.

WISCONSIN

ARCHDIOCESE OF MILWAUKEE

Chancery Office
3501 South Lake Dr.
P.O. Box 07912
Milwaukee, WI 53207–0912
Telephone: (414) 769–3340

ARCHIVIST:
Timothy D. Cary

AREA INCLUDED IN DIOCESE:
Dodge, Fond du Lac, Kenosha, Milwaukee, Ozaukee, Racine, Sheboygan, Walworth, Washington, and Waukesha counties.

Sacramental records for the Archdiocese of Milwaukee have been microfilmed by the Genealogical Society of Utah and are available for viewing at the Family History Library in Salt Lake City and its family history centers, including the family history center at Hales Corner (9600 West Grange Ave., Hales Corner, WI 53130; telephone: (414) 425–4182). Requests to the archdiocese should be by mail.

FEES:
Minimum of $5.00 per research request.

DICOESAN HISTORY:
Milwaukee Catholicism: Essays on Church and Community (1994) by Steven M. Avella (editor).

Centennial Essays for the Milwaukee Archdiocese 1843–1943 (1943) by Rev. Peter Leo Johnson, DD.

CATHOLIC NEWSPAPER:
The Catholic Herald
P.O. Box 07913
Milwaukee, WI 53207

Est. 1869. First title *The Star of Bethlehem* (there have been several name changes). Microfilms are available at the Milwaukee Public Library and *The Catholic Herald* offices.

DIOCESE OF GREEN BAY

Archives
P.O. Box 23066
Green Bay, WI 54305–3066
Telephone: (920) 435–4406

ARCHIVIST:
Sr. Ella J. Kaster

AREA INCLUDED IN DIOCESE:
Brown, Calumet, Door, Florence, Forest, Kewaunee, Langlade, Manitowoc, Marinette, Menominee, Oconto, Outagamie, Shawano, Waupaca, Waushara, and Winnebago counties.

All sacramental records for the diocese are on microfiche at the archives office located at the chancery. The archives also holds the death records for the parishes and microfilm of the diocesan newspaper, *The Compass*. The archivist does research for individuals as time permits. On a limited basis, individuals may come in and use the microfiche records. The University of Wisconsin at Green Bay and the Register of Deeds Office for Brown County have some records from St. John the Evangelist Church in Green Bay. St. John's is the oldest continuously existing parish in Wisconsin; some of its records go back to the 1830s. A number of parishes have published histories or anniversary booklets, many of which are on file at the archives.

FEES:
A $10.00 per hour donation is asked for research that is done for individuals.

DIOCESAN HISTORY:
In his Vineyard (1983). Short biographies of all diocesan priests who served in the diocese.

The Diocese of Green Bay: A Centennial (1968). A semi-picture book format; brief and accurate.

History of the Catholic Church in Wisconsin (1894). Old, sometimes very helpful to researchers, but not always accurate.

CATHOLIC NEWSPAPER:
The Compass
P.O. Box 23825
Green Bay, WI 54305

Est. 1956. Microfilms are located at the diocesan archives and at the Brown County Public Library.

DIOCESE OF LA CROSSE

3710 East Ave. South
P.O. Box 4004
La Crosse, WI 54602–4004
Telephone: (608) 788–7700

AREA INCLUDED IN DIOCESE:
Adams, Buffalo, Chippewa, Clark, Crawford, Dunn, Eau Claire, Jackson, Juneau, La Crosse, Marathon, Monroe, Pepin, Pierce, Portage, Richland, Trempealeau, Vernon, and Wood counties.

Sacramental records for the diocese are maintained at the parish level. Requests for information may be directed to the parish, if known. The diocese can often help in locating a parish if sufficient information is provided.

FEES:
None

DIOCESAN HISTORY:
Dusk is My Dawn (1968) by Rev. Gerald E. Fisher.

CATHOLIC NEWSPAPER:
The Times Review
P.O. Box 4004
La Crosse, WI 54602-4004

Est. 1936 as the *La Crosse Register*, changed to *Times Review* around 1978. Microfilm for the first twenty-five to thirty years is in the Diocesan Archives in La Crosse. There is no microfilm in public libraries. Papers may be researched at the newspaper offices, with limits and regulations. There are no marriages or obituaries in this paper.

DIOCESE OF MADISON

3577 High Point Rd.
Madison, WI 53744
Telephone: (608) 821–3000

Mailing Address:
P.O. Box 44893
Madison, WI 53744

AREA INCLUDED IN DIOCESE:
Columbia, Dane, Grant, Green, Green Lake, Iowa, Jefferson, Lafayette, Marquette, Rock, and Sauk counties.

Sacramental records are maintained at the individual parishes. Supply complete information when requesting records from the chancery or the parish, if known.

FEES:
None.

CATHOLIC NEWSPAPER:
The Catholic Herald
702 N. Blackhawk St.
P.O. Box 5913
Madison, WI 53705

Est. 1948. Bound copies are available at the *Herald* offices for all years. The diocese was created in 1947; before then, the area was covered by the Milwaukee and La Crosse papers. Copies of the *Herald* are available at the Wisconsin State Historical Society and at Edgewood College, both in Madison.

DIOCESE OF SUPERIOR

1201 Hughitt Ave.
P.O. Box 969
Superior, WI 54880
Telephone: (715) 392–2937

AREA INCLUDED IN DIOCESE:

Ashland, Barron, Bayfield, Burnett, Douglas, Iron, Lincoln, Oneida, Polk, Price, Rusk, Sawyer, St. Croix, Taylor, Vilas, and Washburn counties. Sacramental records are maintained at the parish level. Requests should be directed to the parish involved. If precise information is given, the diocese can often provide the name of a parish where records might be located.

FEES:

None.

ADDITIONAL WISCONSIN RESOURCES:

WISCONSIN STATE HISTORICAL SOCIETY

816 State Street
Madison, WI 53706

COLLECTION INCLUDES:

• Microfilms of all newspapers ever published in the state of Wisconsin

UNIVERSITY OF WISCONSIN/ EAU CLAIRE

Library Services 102–089
McIntyre Library
Eau Claire, WI 54702–4004

COLLECTION INCLUDES:

• Church and cemetery records for the eight-county region of the Chippewa Valley (Buffalo, Chippewa, Clark, Eau Claire, Price, Rusk, Sawyer, and Taylor counties.) The collection is not inclusive; it only contains records of churches which participated in the microfilming project
• Birth, death, and marriage records for the area through 1907

UNIVERSITY OF WISCONSIN/ GREEN BAY

7th Floor
Library Learning Center
Green Bay, WI 54301

COLLECTION INCLUDES:

• Records from St. John the Evangelist Church in Green Bay

UNIVERSITY OF WISCONSIN/ LA CROSSE

Murphy Library
1631 Pine Street
La Crosse, WI 54601

COLLECTION INCLUDES:

• Burial records in Norwegian and English for the Catholic Cemetery in La Crosse, generally 1883–1933, on microfilm
• Vital records, 1840s to 1906, for Jackson, La Crosse, Monroe, Trempealeau, and Vernon counties

WYOMING

DIOCESE OF CHEYENNE

Chancery Office
Box 426
Cheyenne, WY 82003
Telephone: (307) 638–1530

AREA INCLUDED IN DIOCESE:

The entire state of Wyoming and Yellowstone
National Park.

Very early records for the diocese are stored at the
Cathedral for the Diocese of Cheyenne. More recent
records are stored in the parishes. Diocesan records
are confidential. They are made available for individuals who have a legitimate need on a case-by-
case basis. A history of the diocese is in progress.

DIOCESAN CEMETERY:

Olivet Catholic Cemetery, Sexton Office
2501 Seymour Ave.
Cheyenne, WY 82002

Records from 1868 to the present are located at the
sexton's office. Microfilm copies of the records are
also located at the Wyoming State Archives in
Cheyenne.

FEES:

None.

WYOMING STATE ARCHIVES/RESEARCH DIVISION

2301 Central Ave.
Cheyenne, WY 82002

COLLECTION INCLUDES:

• Microfilm of Olivet Catholic Cemetery records
• *Wyoming Churchman*, various copies
• Funeral home records (scattered)

SHERIDAN COUNTY

Fulmer Public Library
Sheridan, WY 82801

COLLECTION INCLUDES:

• *Holy Name Centennial*, 1885–1985
• Local funeral home files

ARCHDIOCESE FOR MILITARY SERVICES, U.S.A

962-Wayne Ave.
Silver Spring, MD 20910
Telephone: (301) 853–0400

AREA INCLUDED IN DOICESE:

All U.S. military bases worldwide, including the U.S. Military Academy at West Point, New York, the U.S. Air Force Academy at Colorado Springs, Colorado, the U.S. Naval Academy at Annapolis, Maryland, and the U.S. Coast Guard Academy at New London, Connecticut.

The Archdiocese for Military Service (formerly known as the Military Ordinariate or Military Vicariate) was founded in 1917 to serve active and reserve military personnel of the United States and their dependents. The archdiocese maintains the records of sacraments performed on U.S. military bases worldwide.

DIOCESES MICROFILMED BY THE GENEALOGICAL SOCIETY OF UTAH

As noted in the Introduction, The Genealogical Society of Utah has microfilmed the records of a number of Catholic dioceses. Copies of these microfilms are available through the Family History Library in Salt Lake City, Utah, and through its family history centers located throughout North America.

- Diocese of Buffalo, New York
- Archdiocese of Chicago, Illinois (including cemetery indexes)
- Diocese of Corpus Christi, Texas
- Diocese of El Paso, Texas (partial)
- Diocese of Evansville, Indiana
- Diocese of Fort Wayne-South Bend, Indiana

- Diocese of Gary, Indiana
- Archdiocese of Indianapolis, Indiana
- Archdiocese of Lafayette, Indiana
- Diocese of Kansas City-St. Joseph, Missouri (partial)
- Archdiocese of Milwaukee, Wisconsin
- Archdiocese of Newark, New Jersey
- Diocese of New Ulm, Minnesota
- Diocese of Ogdensburg, New York
- Diocese of Rochester, New York
- Archdiocese of St. Louis, Missouri
- Archdiocese of Santa Fe, New Mexico
- Diocese of Spokane, Washington
- Diocese of Wilmington, Delaware

INDEX OF ARCHDIOCESES AND DIOCESES